Dolphin

Animal
Series editor: Jonathan Burt

Dolphin

Alan Rauch

REAKTION BOOKS

In Memoriam: Brigitte, Fanny, & Judith,
Residents of the Montréal Aquarium, c. 1967–1980

Published by
REAKTION BOOKS LTD
33 Great Sutton Street
London EC1V ODX, UK
www.reaktionbooks.co.uk

First published 2014
Copyright © Alan Rauch 2014

Printed and bound in China by C&C Offset Printing Co., Ltd

A catalogue record for this book is available from the British Library

ISBN 978 1 78023 089 4

Contents

Preface

About 35 million years ago, the creatures we now know as dolphins abandoned the security of land for a life entirely in the ocean. It seems as unlikely an evolutionary move as one can imagine, but it was obviously a successful one; only 10 million years later dolphins became essentially the same creatures as they are now, and they are still going strong. By contrast, human precursors only began to emerge 2 million years ago and *Homo sapiens* did not appear until a few hundred thousand years ago. Bipedal and quintessentially earthbound, humans occupied a world foreign from their cetacean 'cousins', and so, it would seem, there was every reason for the two groups to be oblivious to each other's existence. And yet, despite the fact that humans and dolphins developed in what might be called these two solitudes, the dolphin is one of the most beloved animals in human history.

The paradox of the association between humans and dolphins is not simply that dolphins are totally aquatic animals whose environment necessarily prevents the kind of companionship – and even mutual knowledge – that humans share, say, with dogs. The divergence between these two groups is even more fundamental in that the very traits that all mammals supposedly have in common – hair, mammary glands and even general body shape – have either disappeared or are entirely concealed in cetaceans. The fact that biology teachers and aquaria staff feel obliged to repeat, to

A bottlenose dolphin performing.

all who will listen, that 'the dolphin *is* a mammal', underscores how completely alien these creatures can appear to us.

Yet in the esteem of the public at large, even among individuals who appear to be completely indifferent to animals, dolphins are almost universally beloved. With very rare exceptions, dolphins hardly ever get a bad press and when they do, humans accept the blame for having put them in captivity or for creating unacceptable environmental stresses.

Dolphins are, in a word, charismatic. They seem to 'have it all': intelligence, good looks, refinement and a winning (if not voluntary) smile. And, as anthropomorphic as these perceptions may be, they are not easily refuted. The difficulty stems, in part, from how little we know about dolphin biology, behaviour and communication. Scientific research has made considerable strides in the last five decades, but ultimately dolphins make their home at sea, where humans are, relatively speaking, clumsy. In captivity (a thorny issue in its own right), their 'intelligence' impresses us enough to pursue ethical standards with regard to welfare and research, in contrast to some of the unfeeling techniques used in the past.

As much as we tout human–dolphin companionability, there are serious blemishes in our track record with these animals. Foremost among our faults in studying dolphins (and this might be said of virtually all animals) is that they are not, as we once thought, puzzles to be 'solved'. These are animals, not puzzles, and there are no answers at the back of the dolphin book to confirm or refute our findings. Rather, we have in the dolphin a very real and complex organism that defies the neat and idyllic image that humans have constructed for it. The purpose of this small book is to engage that complexity in as many different ways as possible and to explore our shared fascination and appreciation of the group called dolphins.

A dolphin sculpture, constructed of lemons and oranges, created for the annual Lemon Festival in the French coastal town of Menton.

Much of the dolphin's reputation, in terms of its relationship with humans, has been predicated on four factors: intelligence, aesthetics, proximity and disposition. While the idea of what intelligence actually means has never been (and surely will never be) resolved, the idea that dolphins are socially and cognitively complex creatures is central to our understanding of them. When we see them out at sea they are often travelling in large groups (pods), and no less often 'hitching a ride' on the bow waves of boats and ships. What's more, dolphins can be highly vocal and clearly seem to be communicating, often raucously, with each other, if not also with us. We may not have an adequate working definition of the term, but dolphins do appear to be very 'intelligent'.

As for aesthetics, it's hard to imagine a more elegantly shaped creature. The aquatic environment has contributed to the sleek, hydrodynamic form of dolphins, rendering their form beautifully (and deceptively) simple. The form of dolphins, of course, has more to do with physics than it does with aesthetics, but the two forces work in tandem from a human perspective. We are also deceived, when we look at dolphins, by the curved shape of their mouths that makes them appear to be smiling: that smile is permanent and masks the mood of even the angriest dolphin, but overall it is a trait that endears the animals to us even further. We have long known that they are mammals and that they not only nurse their young, born singly like most human babies, but are painstaking in the care, attention and time they devote to their offspring.

For all the similarities that humans share with these fellow mammals, there is also a remarkable conundrum that presents itself whenever we observe them, and that is that they are not proximate. You can't get really close to a dolphin without getting into the water yourself! Dolphins spend their entire lives in the ocean, we on land. They are, in the parlance of marine biology, 'obligate' ocean dwellers. And the ocean, at least from the perspective of a terrestrial mammal like the human, is a seriously hostile environment. To coin a phrase: it's a nice place for a mammal to visit,

Pernetty's dolphin, now known as the Atlantic spotted dolphin (*Stenella frontalis*), from William Jardine's *The Naturalist's Library* (1837).

The common dolphin porpoising.

but one wouldn't want to live there. It is cold and wet and one must always be on the move to survive. There's nothing for bipeds, like us, or quadrupeds, like the dolphin's ancestors, to stand on, and precious air is only available at the not-always-tranquil surface. And so it is very difficult for us to comprehend what it must be like for these very engaging creatures to live in an environment so unforgiving to us. And this, no doubt, is part of the endless fascination we have with dolphins. It's not that they are 'like' us (they aren't) or even that they actually seem to like us (some may; most are indifferent at best); rather, the attraction for humans may well be that they are, in so many fundamental ways, completely unlike us.

Interpreting the 'disposition' of any animal is a losing proposition, beginning too often with anthropocentric platitudes and ending in fairy-tale narratives. New Age depictions of dolphins often posit them as a kind of alien form among us, as though their role on the planet is to teach humans to be better citizens of Earth; that is, to ostensibly be more like *them*. But this spiritualist vision, compelling though it may be to many, undermines so much of the fascinating reality of dolphins, whose evolutionary transition and adaptation to the world's oceans and rivers is perhaps one of the most intriguing chapters of evolution. To 'become' dolphins, a group of early terrestrial animals underwent significant incremental changes to their anatomy, physiology, biochemistry and behaviour, ultimately rendering them seaworthy. From seemingly mundane adaptations such as developing a layer of insulating blubber or the formation of an elegant tail (the flukes are the only source of propulsion in these creatures), to a system of echolocation that outstrips any comparable human technology, there is no feature of these animals that doesn't either amaze or perplex the human observer. And all of these adaptations are the consequence of one of our ancestral fellow mammals returning to the sea.

1 Zoology and Physiology: Evolution and Adaptation

The ocean teems with life, no one can watch the Flying-fish,
Dolphin & Porpoises without pleasure.
Charles Darwin, *Beagle* diary (1835)

For all we believe we know about dolphins, the question 'What is a dolphin?' is critical to beginning any consideration of the group. Given the very loose usage of terms such as porpoise, whale and dolphin, there has been a lot of popular confusion about what distinguishes one group from the next. This is a complex question as even evolutionary scientists have not quite determined the precise relationships among various species and scholarly discussions about reclassification are taking place even you read these words.

One minor source of confusion, which can be eliminated quickly, concerns the brilliantly coloured dolphin fish (*Coryphaena hippurus*), better known to most people as the mahi-mahi or dorado. This colourful and blunt-headed fish, whose brow can be said to resemble the dolphin's forehead, or melon, is widely distributed, particularly in tropical and subtropical seas, and has become a common item on many restaurant menus, often causing a little consternation amongst diners. But unless one is a vegetarian, there is no need for concern: the *Coryphaena* is a fish, whereas the dolphin is a mammal. Another point of confusion worth clearing up here and now is the panoply of colours the dolphin displays as it dies into dullness. The beautiful 'colours of the dying dolphin' has become a trope for many writers, many of whom were unfamiliar with

dolphins of any kind. Lord Byron, for example, evoked the image
in 'Childe Harold's Pilgrimage':

> . . . parting day
> Dies like the dolphin, whom each pang imbues
> With a new colour as it gasps away,
> The last still loveliest, till – 'tis gone – and all is gray.[1]

Byron probably knew that his dolphin was the fish *Coryphaena*,
but many writers clearly – and mistakenly – have the mammalian 'dolphin' in mind when this dramatic image is invoked.

Aside from this one minor exception, all dolphin species are
mammals and all belong to a larger group, the Order Cetacea,
which includes a remarkable variety of toothed and baleen
whales. The Greeks used the term Ketos to describe large marine

creatures – predominantly whales – and contemporary taxonomy adapted the Latin form of the word, Cetus, to establish a category for all marine mammals including the dolphins.

Before going any further on the subject of mammalian dolphins, it is worth mentioning a couple of interrelated terms that come up a great deal when considering dolphin physiology. The first is the 'rete mirabile', or 'miraculous net'. The rete, though critical to dolphins, can be found in most mammals. It is essentially a maze of arteries and veins that lie very close to each other. This maze or net has two functions, the first being that it can reduce the very forceful flow of blood, which could potentially be damaging to a sensitive organ like the brain, to a manageable level of pressure. Second, the net of the rete mirabile occurs at a scale that allows heat, chemicals and gasses to be exchanged across adjacent capillaries.

The second term, 'countercurrent exchange', describes the process of certain kinds of transfer at a variety of levels, but often at the scale where retia mirabilia may play a significant role. When a system of veins and arteries are arranged so that they are adjacent, warmth from arterial flow can be transferred to cold blood (venous flows) as it returns from the exterior surface of an animal back to the body's core. Without such a mechanism, it would be impossible for dolphins to keep a constant core temperature. At even more minute levels, where either membranes or the cell walls of capillaries are thin enough to be semi-permeable, other materials such as oxygen can be exchanged. In short, it is a kind of regulating system that prevents heat, gasses or chemicals from accumulating at levels injurious to the animal.

At the risk of being tedious, a few general principles of evolutionary history and biology are also worth recapitulating. It is worth remembering, for example, that the first mammals evolved, from a group of reptiles known as synapsids, about 125 million

A porposing bottlenose dolphin with a remora attached.

years ago. The synapsids were all terrestrial creatures, which eventually shared the common characteristics we find in all true modern mammals. The group or class that we call mammals can be categorized by five major characteristics: they breathe air; they produce hair, which is not only good for warmth but an excellent tactile mode – as with whiskers – for sensing one's environment; they have a four-chambered heart, an efficient design that helps maintain a constant temperature through the regular flow of oxygen in the body; they have a placental structure rather than an external egg, to nourish the foetus and then give birth to their young live; they feed their young milk, which is produced in females by the mammary glands.

Aside from hair, all the above traits are easily observed or identified in every marine mammal. Some marine mammals – seals and polar bears, for example – have conspicuous and highly functional hairy pelts. Seals have beautiful coats of fur and

Hair follicles on the rostrum of a bottlenose dolphin.

have been hunted for their pelts for centuries. Dolphins (and whales), however, have no fur and seemingly no visible hair. Even the African naked mole rat (*Heterocephalus glabor*) is anything but hairless, having whisker-like hairs not only on its muzzle but also along the length of its body. The smooth skin of dolphins renders them even more 'naked' than the mole rat, yet on closer observation, hair follicles can been seen on the snout or beak of most young dolphins, and some species even show a few whiskers. Whether or not it is observable now, fur was a prominent trait in early dolphin ancestors, but as they moved from land to water, hair was quickly lost with the need to be as streamlined as possible to enable them to swim rapidly with minimum levels of drag. What did evolve below the skin, or integument, to insulate these hairless creatures was a substantial layer of blubber, which contains lipids (fats) and collagen (a fibrous connective protein). Only the flippers, the flukes and

Anatomy:
in addition to
a layer of blubber,
a dolphin has a
'subdermal sheath'
of connective tissue
that helps put
added energy
into the tail
movements.

the dorsal fins of cetaceans are not protected by a thick layer of blubber, although an insulating layer is always present.

As part of the streamlining effect, in the female the mammary glands are tucked away on either side of what is called, in both males and females, the 'urogenital' slit. Males are equally streamlined. The penis, generally held inside the body, extends through the slit during copulation, while the testes remain in the abdominal cavity, behind the kidneys. Males are distinguished by having a separate anal opening behind the urogenital slit. Dolphin offspring, like the young of most marine mammals, are relatively large, and at birth may weigh as much as one-tenth of the mother's weight. This adaptation is not only necessitated by the cold environment into which they are born but exists so that the young are able to move and swim about immediately. Because dolphin calves do not have lips with which to suckle, the nipples of a nursing female protrude and milk is, through muscular contractions, forcibly expressed into the young dolphin's mouth. Compared to that of terrestrial mammals, cetacean milk is generally very high in fat and protein, helping to accelerate the growth of juvenile animals. According to Kristi West, a biologist working on *Tursiops* (bottlenose dolphins) at the University of Hawaii, 'milk fat doubles from around 10 per cent fat at the beginning of lactation to more than 20 per cent fat by the time calves are weaned. (At 20 per cent fat content, dolphin milk is much thicker and richer than cow's milk.).'[2] West also notes that 'the amount of protein increases over lactation'.

A necessary distinction between cetaceans and land mammals is that the young of cetaceans are born tail first (what obstetricians call breech birth), rather than head first. The logic of this mammalian 'turnaround' is clear from an adaptive perspective, given that land mammals have the luxury of being born directly into the air, whereas cetaceans are born underwater and must swim up to the surface for their first breath. The tail therefore emerges first, leaving the head and the blowhole to appear once the newborn has achieved some mobility, and other attending dolphins (the so-called 'aunts') are able to push the infant towards the surface.

And of course, as members of the family of true mammals, all of which have placentas to support their young, dolphins have belly-buttons! As anyone will know who has seen a dolphin approach an aquarium window, the dolphin navel, which is a little puckered area halfway up the dolphin's underside, is generally easier to spot than the navels of even our domestic animals, such as dogs and cats. It is striking to point the navel out to young (and even older) visitors, who seem surprised yet fascinated to learn that this universal mammalian mark is apparent even in dolphins. While aquaria have added more 'serious' information to their dolphin performances beyond simply scripted shows, visitors can still walk away with little fundamental knowledge about the animals.

A scripted dolphin
performance
with costumed
performers.

The entire order Cetacea, whether baleen whales (Mysticeti) or toothed whales (Odontoceti), share all the characteristics described thus far. But we are strictly interested in a specific group of toothed whales: the family Delphinidae, the dolphins. The dolphin family is diverse and complex, and even though we are familiar with quite a few members of the group, such as the bottlenose dolphin, the spinner dolphin, the killer whale and the pilot whale, there are many less familiar species, such as the slightly larger Risso's dolphin. Current taxonomic charts – which

An upside-down
dolphin showing
the location of
the navel.

Risso's dolphin (below) and a long-finned pilot whale (above) from Buffon's *Natural History*.

are always subject to change as new studies help clarify both genetics and distribution – indicate that there are about 36 species of dolphins, distributed among seventeen genera. As mammalian groups go, dolphin species are not only common worldwide but they are in fact very diverse. By way of comparison, we can look at deer, which comprise another successful mammalian family (Cervidae). There are 44 species in the deer family (including white-tailed deer and reindeer), which are also grouped in seventeen genera. But as diverse and ubiquitous as deer may be, even they are not nearly as widely distributed as the dolphin family. At the opposite extreme, the dolphin's closest living relative, the Hippopotamidae, have only two species extant in two separate genera. And both the large river hippo (*Hippopotamus amphibius*) and the pygmy hippo (*Hexaprotodon liberiensis*) are restricted to the African continent.

Before addressing the diversity of animals linked together as Delphinidae, it is appropriate to begin by asking the fundamental question: what makes a dolphin a dolphin? That is, what distinguishes it from whales in general and from other 'smaller' marine mammals such as the porpoise? Dolphins, to reiterate, are part of the much larger group Cetacea, which is composed wholly of animals whose entire life cycle takes place entirely in the water.[3] Dolphin taxonomy, as we shall see, can be somewhat complex. Oddly enough, one of the consistent features among dolphins is the shape of their teeth, which are in general conical, as opposed to the teeth of porpoises, which are flattened, or 'spatulate'. The tooth count, usually a diagnostic feature in mammals, not only varies across dolphin species but even within individual species. Generally speaking, however, a bottlenose dolphin will have around 86 teeth, with roughly 40 in the upper jaw and 46 in the lower. Since dolphins do not chew their food but simply use their teeth to seize and hold prey, they have no molars and all their teeth are similarly conical ('homodont'). Porpoises are typically smaller than dolphins and do not have the prominent beak, or rostrum, that many dolphin species do. Their dorsal fins also appear more triangular than those of most dolphins, which tend to be falcate, or sickle-shaped. Porpoises appear to be less socially complex and, while they have the ability to echolocate, are much less vocal. In his *Natural History*, Pliny the Elder noted the similarities between porpoises and dolphins but commented that 'porpoises are distinguished from them by a certain gloomy air as they lack the sportive nature of a dolphin'.[4] Pliny's certainty aside, the terms 'dolphin' and 'porpoise' were often used interchangeably throughout the twentieth century, leading to more than a little confusion.

It may be worth looking back into geological time to understand the arrangement of dolphins and whales in general – in other words, the group or order that we call Cetacea. All cetaceans seem to have evolved from a common set of land-dwelling ancestors that occupied the marshy river channels of what was called the Tethys Seaway – the body of water that is now roughly in the location of the Indian Ocean – around 48 million years ago. Recent molecular evidence indicates that the earliest precursor to whales, the recently discovered *Indohyus*,[5] came from a family of early artiodactyls (two-toed creatures) called Raoellidae that resembled small deer. Although a terrestrial creature in appearance, the *Indohyus* would take refuge in the coastal waters of the Tethys Sea when threatened. A contemporary animal comparable to the *Indohyus* is the water chevrotain (*Hyemoschus aquaticus*) or fanged deer, which is an accomplished swimmer with slitted nostrils that often seeks the cover of shallow water when escaping from a predator. A slightly earlier group, the Pakicetids (53 million years ago, in the Eocene), displays characteristics distinctive of later cetaceans, including the structure of the bones of the ear and triangular, serrated teeth, which bear a strong resemblance to the teeth of modern cetaceans. And among the many recent discoveries in Pakistan are the fossil remains of *Ambulocetus*, which some palaeontologists describe as a combination between a mammal and a crocodile and which, along with the hoofed *Pakicetus*, was one of the transitional forms between the land dwellers of the shallow tropical waters of the Tethys and later, fully aquatic forms. Although probably fully comfortable in the water, they were still equipped with rudimentary but functional hind legs, and climbed out of the water to mate and give birth.

To get a sense of these early cetaceans it is well worth thinking again about the hippopotamus, the living mammals to which dolphins are most closely related. Hippos are enormous creatures (up to 4,500 kg, or 5 tons) that spend a considerable amount of time in the water and have clearly adapted to the similar environmental constraints that helped shape dolphins and whales. Hippopotamus nostrils have a valve-like system that keeps the nasal passage shut tight while they swim underwater. They are

An early dolphin ancestor, Indohyus.

gregarious creatures, and their eyes are well adapted to vision both under and above water. They have very little hair and enjoy a layer of insulation about 5 cm (2 in) thick, of fat. In short, we can see some qualities of early cetaceans within the hippopotamus that bear interesting similarities to their distant cousins, the modern cetaceans.

As early cetaceans developed, they began to show adaptations better suited to a life experienced entirely, or almost entirely, in the water. Various groups of wholly aquatic species emerged or radiated in the Eocene period, reflecting a remarkably diverse group of animals. Many, including a group called the Protocetidae, remained amphibious, but the more successful Archaeocetes, the suborder that includes most of the early whales, had committed fully to aquatic life.

The later Archaeocetes were prolific, but despite their initial success they are now entirely extinct. Fossils reveal that their skull structure was less elongated than that of their odontocete

cousins, thus their nostril(s) were at the tip of the rostrum, as they are in alligators and crocodiles. They also still shed a set of baby teeth prior to developing permanent adult teeth, which no longer occurs in odontocetes. The best-known Archaeocete is probably *Basilosaurus*, an 18-metre-long (60 ft) creature of the late Eocene (40 million years ago); an enormous serpentine animal, it acquired the suffix 'saurus' because scientists originally believed it to be a reptile. The hind legs of these animals, though no longer connected (or weakly connected) to the spine, are believed to have been used to clasp partners when mating.

The Archaeocetes also included a group called the Dorudontinae, which eventually divided into the two current sub-orders of whales, the Mysticeti and the Odontoceti, the baleen and the toothed whales. As these orders were emerging simultaneously, they began to show very different skull structures from the Archaeocetes, particularly in the movement of the nostrils towards the top of the head, away from the mouth. The migration of the nostrils to the top of the head allowed for a horizontal posture in the water, so that the animals could rapidly take a breath of air and just as rapidly release it, thereby minimizing 'time spent at or above the surface'.[6] Odontocetes went one step further in refining the process by consolidating the two nasal passages into a single nostril, called a 'spiracle' by very early naturalists, that requires only one valve. Baleen whales, however, retain both nostrils. The importance of not allowing any seepage of water into the respiratory tract, much less the lungs, was critical for both groups, resulting in highly efficient valve systems in all cetaceans.

As a side note here, there appears to be strong evidence that as dolphins get older or become infirm, seepage becomes much more of a problem and the consequence is frequently pneumonia, which is inevitably fatal. Pneumonia, as we know from its human form in hospitals and nursing homes, is a rapid and devastating illness that leaves an unmistakable mark on the lungs, but it is often secondary to some other illness that caused the initial decline in health. Unfortunately, the actual cause of death in captive or beached animals is often overlooked, having been rendered moot by pneumonia. Our knowledge about dolphin pathology, both in captivity and the wild, is thus less accurate than it might be.

One of the adaptations necessary to live in a heavily saline environment is a way to maintain a normal level of salinity in bodily fluids. Shipwrecked sailors facing severe thirst at sea were taught not to indulge in 'mariposa', the voluntary drinking of seawater, because the momentary refreshment gained by a quick drink of seawater inevitably leads to further dehydration due to high levels of salt. The issue is no less of a problem for marine mammals. Dolphins have what appears to be a remarkable set of kidneys, but while they are very efficient they do not seem to concentrate salinity greater than the level of seawater itself.[7] What this means, first and foremost, is that dolphins are clearly not able to ingest seawater and process it efficiently enough, as some seals can, to extract fresh water. So dolphins obtain fresh water by other means, primarily through the foods they consume, sometimes referred to as 'metabolic water'. Fish, squid and crustacea must all maintain a level of non-saline fluids in their systems, and dolphins capitalize on their hard work to maintain their own osmotic balance. There is also evidence that water can transfer over the surface of the skin, and so a dolphin swimming in water with a reduced level of salinity might actually be able to absorb fresh water. Coastal dolphins that occupy estuaries and even intracoastal waterways may therefore derive a double benefit, first from the water in which they swim and second from foods that themselves are less saline. Finally, dolphins have very well-developed tongues, which 'play an important role in squeezing water out of the mouth', a critical adaptation given that any ingestion of food must necessarily be accompanied by a healthy dose of seawater. Anyone who has witnessed a dolphin's remarkable ability to squirt water powerfully and accurately must

The *Basilosaurus,* a 60-foot archaeocete dating back 40 million years.

The blowhole or nostril of a bottlenose dolphin. A valve flap seals the nostril when the dolphin is underwater.

be impressed by the capacity of the mouth to hold water and the ability of the tongue to direct it. Dolphins may in fact use this squirting talent to divert sand away from bottom-dwelling prey, and the flexible tongue may even facilitate nursing in infant dolphins. Keeping in mind that seawater is cold as well as salty, it is not surprising that the tongue is also equipped with counter-current vessels to prevent heat loss when it opens its mouth.

Since dolphins are incapable of chewing their food, they must be selective about the varieties of fish they consume. Because fish can be rough and spiny, dolphins generally reposition food using their tongues, so that fish are swallowed head first. Most of the beaked dolphins capture prey by biting at it, but some species with more rounded heads, like the *Orcaella*, also employ suction feeding; that is, they can create a certain amount of negative pressure by opening up their mouths rapidly, drawing in both water and a fish.[8] In either case, the consumption of fish, to say nothing of squid and shrimp, requires an active digestive system that is equipped to break the meal down – bones, scales and cartilage – as thoroughly as possible. The food that is ingested travels through a fairly complex stomach not unlike the gut system of their artiodactyl relatives (deer and even cows), consisting of a 'front' chamber (or forechamber), a main chamber, as well as two smaller pouches. To aid in digestion, dolphin stomachs are well equipped with bacteria that break down chitin, a cellulose-like material found in a variety of crustaceans. Dolphin intestines are extremely long in order to facilitate as much absorption of fluids (from the digested food) as possible, as well as to extract the maximum amount of nutrition.

HEAT RETENTION

Dolphins, like other marine mammals, face serious challenges as warm-blooded creatures living in a cold environment. Surrounded by water, which is always wicking away (as it were) core body temperature, dolphins must retain their body heat. An effective barrier to the cold is the layer of blubber that surrounds the dolphin just below the initial layers of skin. Blubber is a lipid-rich layer of fat that varies in thickness and that ultimately contributes to the streamlined shape of all cetaceans. Blubber also plays a critical role in keeping these muscular animals buoyant. Structured throughout with collagen fibres and blood vessels, the blubber layer simultaneously holds the form of the dolphin and serves as a site for energy (fat) storage and retrieval. When heat retention is needed, blood vessels are constricted, preventing the loss of warmth, but when energy needs to be deposited or retrieved, blood flow returns to 'normal'. Together, the skin and blubber is a remarkable organ that is beautifully adapted to the harsh and frigid conditions of an aquatic environment. But blubber can also be problematic in a very active dolphin that is swimming rapidly, because as muscle temperatures rise with exertion, the animal must prevent itself from overheating inside. A simple analogy, for anyone who has worn a warm overcoat on a cold day, is that while standing still the coat seems a perfect barrier to the cold but if forced to run a long distance the wearer of the coat will quickly become overheated.

Fortunately, the dolphin has a very effective system of counter-current circulation that can allow for the transfer and retention of heat. In this physiological system, blood vessels are arranged adjacent to each other so that the warmth of blood being pumped from the heart can elevate the temperature of blood that has been cooled from circulating near the dolphin's extremities. Both the fins and the flukes of a dolphin also play an important role in controlling temperature. If overheated, blood can be easily cooled by being diverted into dorsal fin and flukes, which are not layered in blubber. Elephants use their broad and very thin ears in a similar fashion.

DIVING PHYSIOLOGY

Dolphins, particularly open-water ('pelagic') species, are capable of diving for extended periods and to relatively extensive depths. The bottlenose dolphin, for example, is known to be able to dive to 535 metres (1,750 ft), although under natural conditions, dives are typically 3 to 45 metres (10–150 ft). The stresses placed on an animal through diving are considerable. Deep dives require a substantial length of time (often 10 minutes) and subject the animal to significant pressure. On land, we all experience a pressure of 14.7 pounds per square inch (psi) of pressure, or 1 'atmosphere', but if we dive in salt water, an additional atmosphere of pressure occurs with every 10 metres (33 ft) of depth. The pressure can be intense, even for the relatively shallow-diving bottlenose dolphin, which at 45 metres encounters 5 atmospheres. Pilot whales have been known to descend to close to 600 metres (2,000 ft), where the water pressure is, for us at least, unimaginable. In what ways have dolphins adapted to accommodate these stressors?

Like humans, dolphins store oxygen in the blood in a protein molecule called haemoglobin. Thus the air we take in through breathing passes from the lungs to the blood and then goes on to provide oxygen to our brains and the rest of our bodies. Because dolphins have, by weight, about three times the amount of blood in their bodies as humans, there is even more storage capacity for oxygen. Moreover, they also store a considerable amount of oxygen, more than any non-diving animals, in 'myoglobin', which can be found in the muscle tissue. Muscles consume a great deal of oxygen when working hard and thus it is useful to have a self-stored supply, rather than to delete oxygen from the blood. The dolphin also conserves oxygen by shutting off the supply of blood to many organs – those which are not critical to diving – thereby conserving oxygen for the brain. Because dolphins are not taking in additional oxygen during a dive, as scuba divers must, there is less concern for nitrogen dissolving into the blood and generating what is typically called 'the bends'.

The concentrated pressure of diving to great depths means that dolphins (and most marine mammals) actually exhale prior to diving, in order to avoid the compression of air into bubbles of gas within the respiratory system. The lungs are therefore not actually exchanging oxygen with the blood, or are doing so at a very limited rate, during a dive. The lungs and the ribcage are in fact very flexible so that they can sustain compression as a dolphin moves to lower depths. Other air sacs, like sinuses, which inconvenience humans during diving, do not exist in dolphins (they are less necessary, as dolphins cannot smell), and ear pressure is abated by a very sturdy bone structure surrounded by fluids that, as we shall see, actually assists in the transmission of sound waves.

Although dolphins do not appear to have necks, they are no different from all other mammals, from mice to giraffes, in having seven cervical, or neck, vertebrae. In some species, such as the bottlenose dolphin, these vertebrae are highly compressed, so they have limited flexibility in the neck. By contrast, some of the freshwater dolphins, which root around on the river bottom and must navigate tight spaces, have relatively flexible necks. Still, since raising the blowhole above the surface is critical, there is an advantage for all dolphins in being able to curve or arch the head. While cervical vertebrae remain constant at seven, the total number of vertebrae in the spine varies from species to species.

LIVING UNDERWATER

The American philosopher Thomas Nagel's famous essay, titled 'What is it Like to Be a Bat?', remains a cornerstone of animal studies, which in some sense is always striving to comprehend the lives of animals – which is, as Nagel concludes, impossible.[9] So, while we can never 'imagine' what it is like to live underwater, it may be a worthwhile exercise to consider some of the evolutionary 'obstacles' necessary in the transition from land to sea. Needless to say, these 'obstacles' were overcome and thus were not, strictly speaking, impediments to the emergence of the cetaceans and ultimately the dolphins, but a quick review (collapsing millions of years in a paragraph or two) will serve as a good introduction to the dolphin as an organism.

The transition to water, from an evolutionary perspective, was so highly complicated a process that it almost defies credulity that a small group of terrestrial mammals actually evolved into a broad group of fully aquatic creatures. It was a move, first of all, into a medium that is '800 times denser and 60 times more viscous than air'.[10] Any reader who swims, does aquatic aerobics or who has simply trudged through the waves to 'frolic' in the ocean, a lake or a pool, knows how much extra energy is required underwater even for the slightest movement. The same reader, immersed up to her/his neck in water, will also quickly become aware of how good the dense medium of water is at reducing body temperature. We may not shiver very much (to keep warm) near the shore, but move 30 metres (100 ft) towards deeper water and the heat loss becomes serious.

Perhaps the greatest advantage of living on land is that terrestrial mammals have the luxury of moving around in air, the very medium they breathe. Dolphins, however, face the constant necessity of having to return to the surface for air in between long stretches of holding their breath below the surface, whether to catch prey or escape predators. Although it seems obvious, let us recall that air, when brought underwater, is inconvenient, because it fills up the lungs, which are then buoyant; this buoyancy is hardly convenient for underwater navigation. For terrestrial mammals, whether diurnal (like humans) or nocturnal (like bats), night and day are clearly delineated. The dark–light distinction for cetaceans is not as simple. Diving from a very sunny and bright surface, a dolphin will begin to lose light rapidly as its depth increases, until there may be almost no light at all. The evolution of echolocation (sonar) has clearly addressed that problem, but simply saying that ignores the enormously complex adaptation needed to produce, receive and process the sounds that make echolocation work. We shall look at this process shortly.

The harsh aquatic environment has necessitated in all cetaceans a robust countercurrent heat-exchange system, critical to survival. Within that system, networks of retia mirabilia are essential for maintaining comfortable temperatures and appropriate levels of ions and gasses, for an animal's survival. Retia are no less important as buffers against powerful bursts of blood flow, when blood pressure changes dramatically. Giraffes, for example, maintain high blood pressure to keep a strong flow of oxygenated blood reaching the brain. This is well and good when the animal is standing, but when it lowers its head that pressure is intensified further by the gravitational pull downwards, and so to protect the delicate tissues of the brain, blood is shunted through a rete mirabile. One can simply think of a garden hose, which without a nozzle has a strong and regular flow. To prevent the flow from being too powerful, say, when watering plants, you can press your finger against the opening, causing a more gentle spray. Dolphins, which face dramatic changes in pressure as they dive and rise again to the surface, are constantly changing their heart rate and redirecting the flow of blood around their bodies, and so retia are an essential part of their ability to survive.

MOVEMENT AND PROPULSION

Dolphin flukes, which resemble aeroplane wings in both form and function, are a 'key innovation in the evolution of cetaceans'.[11] They are all the more remarkable in that they developed independently of any other structure, such as the hind limbs, as a source of movement. Equally fascinating is that the up and down movement of the flukes involved a fundamental change in the action of the entire body of cetaceans: the change entailed a shift from 'lateral axial undulation' to 'vertical axial undulation'. In other words, most swimming mammals, such as otters, sway their bodies sideways – from left to right – for propulsion. Cetaceans, however, move up and down and have a spine adapted to support the substantial musculature needed to move the flukes vigorously in these directions.[12]

To facilitate swimming, dolphins also have the advantage of what is called 'subdermal connective tissue', which encases the body of the dolphin in a criss-cross pattern. The dolphin, writes the researcher Ann Pabst, 'can be modelled as a fibre-wound, thin-walled, pressurized cylinder'.[13] In short, it is as though each dolphin is fitted internally with a kind of girdle. With each stroke of the tail, the blubber, along with the tightly wound sheath, is stretched; the underside with an upward stroke and the dorsal side with a downward stroke. The tail is thus 'spring-loaded', as it were, and when the stretched portion of the animal returns to 'normal', the tail can take advantage of the potential energy stored in the 'spring'. Given estimates that the cetacean mode of swimming is five times more efficient

The skeleton of a Pacific white-sided dolphin. Note the spinous processes along the back and near the tail that allow for muscle attachment.

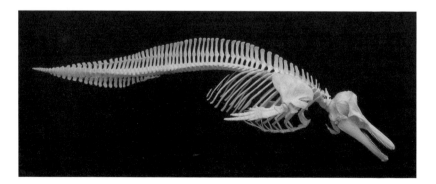

than that of other swimming mammals, this adaptation has been more than beneficial.

The evolution of flukes remains something of a mystery because little or no fluke tissue remains preserved in the fossils we have of early cetaceans. It has been demonstrated, mostly by looking at the development of tails in cetacean embryos, that flukes have nothing to do with the hind legs of their ancestors. Rather, they seem to have developed at the latter part of the tail as a source of power that is more efficient than a pair of paddling feet. Eventually, the hind legs of whales and dolphins became greatly reduced and now they are entirely vestigial, if there are even traces of them at all, in contemporary species. In 2006, a dolphin with what appeared to be the traces of hind limbs was captured in Japan; although there has never been any question about the terrestrial origins of dolphins, the 'limbs' were touted as a 'throwback to [dolphins'] ancient land-dwelling ways'.[14] While all flukes seem to resemble each other in general, there are important variations in the contour of the flukes from species to species.

An interesting perspective on flukes has arisen recently, in the case of Winter, a bottlenose dolphin rescued off the coast of Florida by the staff of the Clearwater Marine Aquarium. Winter's injuries, the consequence of having been caught in a crab trap, were so severe that her flukes and several vertebrae had to be amputated. Winter learned how to swim by swinging her body (and her tail stock or 'caudal peduncle') sideways in a fish-like motion. In spite of this working reasonably well for Winter, there was serious concern about the impact this unnatural motion would have on the spine. Winter's plight became known to Kevin Carroll of the Hanger prosthetics company, who had developed a major reputation in prosthetics and began to design and develop a prosthetic tail for Winter. The rehabilitation process, which is still ongoing, is complicated by finding the right materials for power and flexibility, as well as by the difficulty of coupling a prosthetic to the very sensitive skin of a dolphin. It has also been necessary to create multiple versions of the tail because Winter, only four years old when she was rescued, has continued to grow. The most difficult challenge, assuming the prosthetic is successful, will be retraining Winter to swim by moving her tail up and down in the natural (dorso-ventral) motion. Needless to say, this is a compelling story and it has already been told in the children's book *Winter's Tail: How One Little Dolphin Learned To Swim Again* (2009),[15] as well as in a film, *Dolphin Tale* (2011).

Whatever the configuration of the flukes, there is an upper limit to the speed that any species can attain while swimming; the limiting factor – as I indicated earlier – is based on the amount of heat produced internally by active swimming.[16] To reiterate briefly, muscle activity produces heat and any substantial or prolonged rise in temperature risks damage to internal organs. Humans deal with excess heat by sweating, a process that is facilitated in athletes by low body fat so that heat can be released at the skin's surface without impediment. Still, extreme conditions and onerous tasks (like a marathon) can result in heat exhaustion even for experienced runners with low body fat and a healthy rate of perspiration. But perspiration is certainly not an option for cetaceans, which are constantly surrounded by water, and dolphins must retain a substantial layer of blubber to prevent hypothermia; the blubber layer is a wonderful boundary for preventing the cold from getting in, and the warmth from getting out (except through flukes, fins, flippers and possibly the mouth). The system works beautifully when the animals are not under stress, but when speed is called for (to escape predators, for example), difficulties may arise. Thus dolphins (and

Winter the dolphin without her prosthetic tail.

most cetaceans) seldom swim, at least in any sustained way, at speeds greater than about 40 kilometres per hour (25 mph), which seems to be the upper limit before internal heat can damage the organs.

While the dolphin relies on its flukes for propulsion, the flippers are critical to manoeuvring their way through water. Flippers have no role in propulsion but are used as a 'biological hydroplane', to position or navigate the dolphin; in short, they are used to 'increase lift, reduce drag, execute turns, and enable braking'.[17] Anatomically, the flippers are equivalent to front legs or arms and share the same skeletal structure, so that virtually every cetacean displays the remnants of the original five digits of the front foot or, in the case of humans, the fingers of the hand. Typically the first and fifth digits in the flipper are reduced, while the remaining three digits have developed extra phalanges (finger bones) and thus have become elongated.[18] This process strengthens the leading edge of the flipper, giving the entire structure additional control. The shape of the flipper in various species of dolphin can be very distinctive, from the falcate profile of a bottlenose dolphin's flipper to the very broad and rounded shape of the flippers of the killer whale, to the elongated, almost wing-like form of the pilot whale's. It can be taken for granted that each shape confers some advantage to its bearer, but very little work has been done to understand the actual dynamics of flipper shape, size or mobility.

Like any object moving through space, dolphins experience what is called 'skin friction drag', the resistance of the surrounding water to the animal's body. Compared to air, the medium in which most mammals travel, water is highly viscous and highly resistant. The streamlined, tapered ('fusiform') shape of the dolphin helps reduce drag considerably, as it does in aeroplanes and submarines. Dolphins also improve their hydrodynamic profile by constantly sloughing off their outermost layer of skin, thereby maintaining a very smooth surface close to the water; the process also has the added advantage of keeping the dolphin's skin free of parasites.

When serious speed is called for, dolphins engage in a swimming behaviour termed porpoising, by which they leap in and out of the water repeatedly. The obvious advantage, a consequence of the fact that air is a less resistant medium than water, is that a porpoising dolphin can achieve a certain speed with less drag than a dolphin swimming entirely below the surface. But leaving the water for the aerial portion of porpoising costs energy itself, so dolphins tend to porpoise 'when the cost of leaping from the water becomes smaller than the drag on the animal in water'.[19]

Because porpoising is a rapid, high-energy activity, the dolphins have to breathe more deeply, but this is made simpler by having more time, as it were, in the air. In general, coming to the surface costs energy its own right because of the additional resistance created by the waves at the surface ('wave drag').[20] Thus even if the waters are extremely calm, it is much more efficient (in fact it can be up to five times as efficient) for a dolphin swimming leisurely to remain underwater and so to breathe less frequently. Still, groups of dolphins can be seen gliding along the surface in relatively large numbers, indicating that aside from coming up for air, there are other social benefits to keeping one's head above water.[21]

Efficiency is the bottom line for virtually all animals in the wild, and energy management is always at a premium for swimming animals, so it is not surprising to find dolphins taking advantage of the 'free' energy afforded by the bow waves of boats and ships. By situating themselves on the leading (downward) edge of the wave (as surfers do with natural waves), a dolphin can expend less energy travelling a certain distance than they would otherwise. The fact is, however, that dolphins often travel in large groups, and they can take advantage of similar principles when swimming together, either side-by-side or in what is called 'echelon swimming', in which the arrangement of the animals reduces the drag experienced by other members of the pod. Baby dolphins often take advantage of the 'pull', or draft, generated by their mothers, which works particularly well for them because of their small size.

VISION

There is nothing to suggest, as was once believed, that vision in most dolphins is deficient in any way. In fact, many species need to be able to see relatively well in the air, at the surface and at minor depths in clear water. In rivers, where there is a great deal of turbidity and silt, certain species have highly reduced vision. The susu (genus *Platanista*), also called the blind river dolphin or the side-swimming dolphin and which can be found in Bangladesh, Nepal, Pakistan and India does not have a crystalline lens structure in its eye. This means it is probably only capable of determining the brightness, intensity and direction of light, particularly in the opaque waters of the Indus and the Ganges. Their foraging and movement require an almost constant buzzing of echolocation signals.

We know that visual acuity is important for killer whales and bottlenose dolphins not merely for predatory behaviour but even for recognizing each other and for navigation. Both of these species, as well as many other dolphins and whales, raise their heads above the surface to 'spyhop', by which an animal simply looks around, a behaviour common in the wild. It is not entirely clear what information is being taken in during a spyhop, though it might well include assessing location, evaluating the arrangement of the local pod and monitoring other animals (or boats and flotsam).

Vision in the sea requires some serious adaptations to the eye, which must withstand the saline environment, the intense pressure of dives, and the variation of darkness and light between the surface and the ocean depths. Almost all parts of the dolphin's eye are much thicker than in land animals and thus more resistant to pressure. Blood flow to the eye is controlled by a rete mirabile, which helps regulate temperature changes in the cool waters of the sea. The tear ducts of cetaceans release an oily infusion that protects the eye from the salt water. Bottlenose dolphins are also able to 'pooch' out their eyes (extend the eyes a little further out of the orbit) from their normally flattened state to a

A killer whale spyhopping.

more spherical shape in order to get a stereoscopic view when looking ahead, or to obtain better peripheral vision on either side. Moving the eye out in this way may also improve their vision out of water, particularly for images at a distance.

Because open-water dolphins may move quickly between the brilliant light of the surface and the intense darkness of the depths, the pupil of the eye is capable of moving rapidly from a large oval opening, to allow as much light in as possible, to a very constricted formation that limits the intake of light through what appear to be two small pinholes. Dolphins, like dogs and cats, whose eyes shine at night, also have a tapetum, a reflective surface on the back of the retina that intensifies any light taken in through the pupil. These adaptations that help facilitate and even increase the intake of light suggest that vision is important for dolphins in almost all settings.

Breaching is yet another above-surface behaviour which underscores the visual lives of dolphins. Common among all whales and dolphins, breaching animals leap out of the water and then land hard (or so it seems) on their sides. Breaching has the distinct advantage of being both an auditory and a visual signal. The impact against the water of a breaching dolphin (to say nothing of a killer whale) is loud and can be heard both above and below the surface. At the same time, a breaching animal above the surface may be able to get visual cues about its surroundings. And finally, a breaching or leaping dolphin will itself catch the attention of distant animals through both sight and sound. Nevertheless, the function of breaching is not as simple as we may want to believe; the behaviour might just as easily announce the presence of food or warn against danger, or simply function as a form of play. There is no reason to assume that breaching (or any behaviour for that matter) has a single purpose or that environmental circumstances might be influential in the behaviour. But from a strictly functionalist perspective, it is worth considering that one advantage of breaching is that it may help shake off any parasites, such as whale lice, from the surface of the skin.

Sleep is always a risky behaviour for animals because it increases vulnerability to predation, yet it is also critical for an organism's well-being. Sleeping in a watery environment exacerbates the problem, not only because of the threat of predators. Several forms of sleep and resting behaviour have been observed, but there is probably a lot more to be learned about how dolphins achieve and are refreshed by rest. Because the animals are always exposed to the threat of predation, dolphins (in social groups) tend to take turns sleeping and resting, so that some can doze relatively motionless at the surface while others remain alert to the environment directly around them. This arrangement makes sleep a little less risky if, as it is assumed, there are fellow dolphins fully awake at all times, some perhaps even acting as what might be called sleep 'monitors'.

Although most mammals typically close their eyes to sleep, dolphins appear to sleep with at least one eye open. In effect, dolphins are capable of resting one half of their brains at a time, which makes sense, given that dolphins do not breathe automatically the way that most mammals do. A by-product of living and diving in the water is that dolphins need to be able to control the breathing reflex, and do so consciously. In fact, early attempts to anaesthetize dolphins were disastrous, because once 'under' anaesthetic, the dolphins stopped breathing and those that could not be revived or resuscitated in some way, died. Something similar might happen if a dolphin were to be struck unconscious or, more simply, if it were capable of falling asleep completely as other animals do.

Another resting behaviour is what has been called 'bottom sink', by which an animal (often solitary, at least in captivity) will slowly sink to the bottom without moving a limb or, of course, breathing.[22] The process lasts for a minute or two until the animal seems to come out of its reverie and return to normal behaviour. Bottom sink has been observed more frequently in captivity, but it has been noted in shallow-water dolphins as well.

Dolphins have very sensitive skin and seem to touch each other, with their pectoral fins, dorsal fins and even genitalia, for communication.[23] It is possible that flipper contact serves, on occasion, as a grooming function, but it is equally likely that the contact the dolphins make is a means of establishing social connections within a group. Male dolphins use their genitalia to make contact with other animals in what appear to be non-sexual situations.

While gentle contact may be an important element of play, dolphins are also capable of rougher forms of interaction. Certain signals, such as slapping the flukes on the surface of the water, suggest irritation and may be a warning to other animals. The warning can be follow by a tail slap directed underwater at another animal, which can have considerable impact. Another

Dolphins in playful contact.

gesture expressing displeasure is 'raking', during which a dolphin passes its open mouth across the skin of another animal, leaving a series of tooth marks that appear like stripes across the surface of the skin. Although the marks can last for a long time, the animals generally do not draw blood, and the gesture is rarely repeated. Nor does it appear that dolphins 'ram' each other in the way that they have been seen to ram repeatedly into other animals, notably sharks. Ramming is a defensive gesture that can be very powerful, especially against the cartilaginous bodies of sharks, and it seems to be reserved for predators alone.

Both captive and wild dolphins show evidence of shark attacks, through scarring and sometimes through missing portions of the fluke or the dorsal fin. In warm and temperate waters, dolphins are also subject to attacks from the notorious cookie-cutter shark (*Isistius brasiliensis*), a small oceanic predator that

A prominent scar on a dolphin, probably from a shark bite.

can carve out round chunks of flesh from cetaceans and other fish. Though rarely fatal, the distinctively round wounds from a cookiecutter attack may take some time to heal, and they create the risk of infection, heat loss and attracting other predators. Given how common it is to see scars and nicks on dolphins, there can be no question that injuries, some apparently serious, are experienced frequently. There is surely some kind of support or protection for injured animals within a pod, but given that they receive no medical attention, survival rates are impressive. Recently, studies have begun to look at the dolphin's remarkable ability to heal serious wounds while resisting both pain and infection, although the process of natural recuperation is still not understood.[24] Dolphins, like sharks, also attract the less injurious remora, or sharksucker (*Remora remora*), a fish that attaches itself via suction (using a modified dorsal spine) to the underside of an animal in order to scoop up any debris left from feeding. Remoras are not destructive (unlike the cookiecutter) but are a source of unwanted drag, and dolphins actively breach, spin and jump to dislodge these annoying freeloaders.

It is now commonplace to be reminded by television announcers, teachers, museum or zoo docents, and even by children, that 'We are all mammals'. To be sure, it is useful and sobering to recall the seemingly limitless characteristics, whether physiological, anatomical, or biochemical, that all mammals have in common. Yet it is equally important to consider carefully and methodically – to the extent that we are able – what distinguishes each family within that broad group, to say nothing of each genus and species. We will never, as Thomas Nagel reminds us, be able to fully understand bats, though we work hard to achieve some inkling of what their lives must be like. The zoology and physiology of the dolphins presents no less a challenge and the task of appreciating the remarkable evolutionary twists and turns that resulted in cetaceans may be particularly daunting. But, given that we are so different and yet so alike, how can we not be fascinated? And how can we not persist in the attempt to understand the dolphin's world?

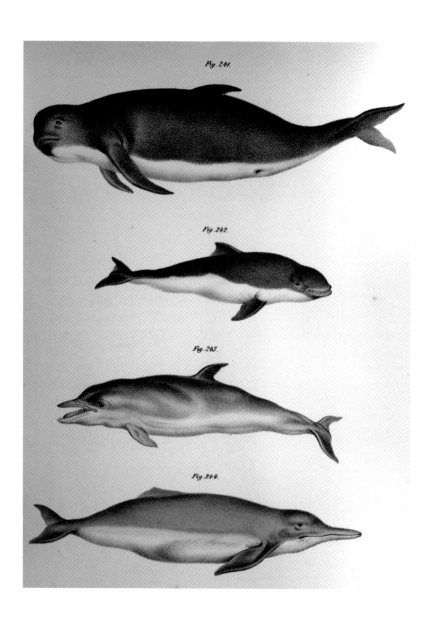

Fig. 241.

Fig. 242.

Fig. 243.

Fig. 244.

2 Species of Dolphin:
A Cosmopolitan Animal

> What object has struck the imagination more than the dolphin? Since man has travelled the vast domains, conquered by his genius, he finds the dolphin on the surface of every sea. He encounters him in the happy climates of temperate zones, under the burning skies of equatorial seas, and in the horrible valleys that separate the mountains of ice that time elevates on the surface of the polar oceans.
>
> Georges-Louis Leclerc, Comte de Buffon, *Histoire Naturelle* (1805)

The term 'dolphin' includes a very diverse group of animals that ranges in size from 1 metre (3 ft) to nearly eight times that length. They can be found in rivers as well as oceans, and are distributed throughout the world. As large mammals go, setting aside rodents and bats, the family Delphinidae comprises more genera and species than most other mammalian groups. There are many field guides devoted to dolphins that describe each species within this impressive variety in meticulous detail. Within the context of these pages, I will only focus on enough species to represent the breadth of the family and to suggest a little something about what distinguishes them.

We already know that dolphins are not porpoises, but the fact is that the common names of some larger dolphins include the word 'whale'. The killer whale, which will be discussed shortly, is perhaps the best example, but this is also true of the pilot whale, genus *Globicephala*, which can reach 6 metres (20 ft) or more in length. Long known to mariners as 'blackfish' or 'pothead whales' for their bulbous 'foreheads', the two existing species of pilot whale are difficult to tell apart and are usually distinguished

The *Grind-Delphin* or Pilot Whale (top) from Leopold Joseph Fitzinger's *Naturgeschichte der saugethierre* (1860). Also shown are the harbour porpoise, the common dolphin and the Amazon dolphin.

51

by the length of their fins, which are narrow and sharply curved back. Originally believed to have been led by a group leader or 'pilot', these dolphins travel in pods of between about twenty and 90 individuals. Mass strandings among pilot whales seem to be more frequent than in any other species, although it is not clear why; the phenomenon of mass stranding, common in a variety of species, is not well understood. The very strong social bonds demonstrated among dolphins may be a contributing factor and it has been proposed that a 'follow-the-leader' mentality may also result in mass strandings. Another possible cause is an infectious disease shared among the pod that in some way disables their ability to navigate. Pilot whales have been kept in captivity and have been trained to perform, but they also become highly agitated in small enclosures and have a very low survival rate.

In addition to the pilot whale, several other delphinids are popularly referred to as whales, including the melon-headed whale (*Peponocephala electra*) which closely resembles the pilot whale, the false killer whale (*Pseudorca crassidens*) and the pygmy killer whale

A pod of pilot whales.

The false killer whale, which belongs to a different genus than the killer whale.

(*Feresa attenuata*). These species are occasionally confused with each other, as they all lack prominent beaks, are generally dark with few distinguishing marks, are all roughly 3–4 metres long (10–13 ft) and have distinctively long flippers. Furthermore, they are all widely distributed in temperate to cool oceans worldwide. Fortunately, identifying one species from the next is facilitated by the differing shape of their dorsal fins.

Dorsal fins are not only helpful in identifying species, but given that they sometimes vary in colour patterns and often reveal nicks, cuts, shark bites and abrasions, they can often be used to distinguish individuals. The only species that do not have dorsal fins are the very sleek right whale dolphins, which can often be seen porpoising in huge groups in the open seas. The absence of the dorsal fin led, no doubt, to their being named after the right whale, which also has no dorsal fin or ridge. It is not clear what hydrodynamic implications, if any, result from the absence of a dorsal fin, although it would certainly lessen the

drag experienced by these dolphins, which are capable of lengthy
dives (over 6 minutes).

The fact that dolphins are so widely distributed and not
readily captured (for research) makes the issue of speciation
and taxonomy problematic. Populations of animals that seemed
to be merely an ecotype or an interesting variation from another
group have recently been reclassified as a separate species. Given
our limited knowledge of dolphins, it is not surprising that a
certain amount of reshuffling of groups as new species or even
as part of a completely different genus occurs. So, for example,
the bottlenose dolphin's close cousin *Tursiops aduncus*, the Indo-
Pacific bottlenose dolphin, which itself was only identified as a
separate species in the 1990s, is now being looked at as a possible
member of the genus *Stenella*. In Australia, another member of
the bottlenose group was reclassified as the Burrunan dolphin
(*Tursiops australis*) after a study of its mitochondrial DNA.[1] The
upshot is that there still remains some fluidity and uncertainty

in dolphin taxonomy and so the number of species within a genus – to say nothing of the number of dolphin species altogether – is likely to shift with time as diagnostic methods become even more sophisticated.

Many species of dolphin are known for their acrobatics, which includes breaching, somersaulting and very pronounced porpoising. For example, the grey-blue Peale's dolphin (*Lagenorhyncus australis*), restricted to the waters off South America and the Falkland Islands, is renowned for its energetic backward leaps. Even more acrobatic than Peale's dolphin is the dusky dolphin (*Lagenorhyncus obscurus*), sometimes called Fitzroy's dolphin, a name bestowed by Charles Darwin to honour Captain Robert FitzRoy, the captain of the HMS *Beagle*. An active jumper, the dusky will leap many times in succession (often with other duskies) and

The Southern right whale dolphin, notable for the absence of a dorsal fin, along with Pacific white-sided dolphins.

slap the water, ostensibly to signal the location of schools of fish or squid to other dolphins.

Among the more distinctive dolphins, with respect to coloration, are the piebald dolphins (*Cephalorhynchus*), which can be found in southern and tropical waters. These dolphins share with orcas a very hard-edged black-and-white pattern which must in some way serve to disrupt the bulk of their form. This fragmented appearance in the piebald's case probably makes them less visible to predators, and for orcas it must make them less visible to prey. All the members of the group are relatively small and light, though stocky in appearance, and are typically coastal. Within this group is the diminutive Commerson's dolphin (*C. commersonii*), often called the skunk dolphin, which can weigh fewer than 27 kilograms (60 lb). Yet despite being one smallest species of dolphin, it is a very active and acrobatic swimmer and is known for swimming upside down (perhaps to spot prey near the surface more precisely).

One of the most esoteric or elusive dolphins is Fraser's dolphin, which was only described on the basis of a skull that Francis Fraser, a cetologist, uncovered in 1956 at London's Natural History Museum. Fraser determined that the dolphin was unique and dubbed it *Lagenodelphis hosei*, and the species has since been observed in the wild, despite having evaded detection until the mid-twentieth century. Considered excellent divers capable of foraging to considerable depths, Fraser's dolphin is still a new enough species to be an enigma to modern cetology.

Another elusive dolphin is the rough-toothed dolphin (*Steno bredanensis*), which can be found worldwide. It is often mistaken for bottlenose and spinner dolphins, but is distinctive in that its 'forehead' slopes straight into the rostrum so that no distinctive beak is apparent. Indeed, mariners often refer to it as 'the slopehead' which, however undignified, is a nickname that is certainly

Peale's dolphin or the 'blackchinned' dolphin.

accurate. For sheer spectacular aerobatics, the spinner dolphins (*Stenella longirostris*) outshine virtually any other group of dolphins. A spinner's leap can take it up to 3 metres in the air and through a remarkable series of spins on its way back down, making it one of the most visible (if not best-known) members of the entire dolphin family. Like its relative the spotted dolphin (*Stenella attenuata*), the spinner is often found in the company of large schools of yellowfin tuna, and both species have suffered serious depredation from purse-seine tuna fisheries.

The striped dolphin (*Stenella coeruleoalba*), a close relative of the spinner, is impressive in its own right. It can leap over 6 metres (20 ft) into the air and they are often seen somersaulting, porpoising in synchrony and even porpoising on their backs. Striped dolphins are known to be deep divers (below 180

Dusky dolphins leaping in apparent play.

metres, 600 feet), which may explain the fact that they have been recorded staying below the surface for as long as ten minutes. Most amateur dolphin watchers are likely to see, at some point, the common dolphin (*Delphinus delphis*), which lives up to its name in that it can be found across the world, from temperate to tropical waters. It is probably one of the most prolific species of dolphin and distinctive because of the yellowish criss-cross pattern on its body. It is also likely to be seen leaping out of the water, perhaps not as impressively as the spinner or striped dolphins, but with a skill that is breathtaking.

Of all of the oceanic dolphins, the one most familiar to us is the bottlenose (*Tursiops truncatus*), if only because it is the dolphin most frequently kept in captivity. There are certainly over 100 bottlenose dolphins currently on display in various aquaria across

A pod of Commerson's dolphin, sometimes called the Piebald dolphin or the Skunk dolphin.

the USA, and more than 2,000 were captured for display between 1972 and 1974. It is not clear how many are currently on display worldwide or the number of animals that are captured annually to sustain populations in captivity. The bottlenose dolphin is the species most widely held in captivity because of its tractability, its comfort in relatively shallow waters, and finally because it is one of the most populous species. Since it is also found in coastal waters throughout the world, from the cold waters of the North Atlantic through virtually all tropical seas, the bottlenose is very flexible and adaptive. One of the larger members of the dolphin family, the bottlenose dolphin easily ranges between 2 and 3.5 metres (6–12 ft) in length, although the larger and no doubt bulkier animals are often in offshore waters.

The bottlenose, because it is so widely distributed and so apparently comfortable living near humans, is the species we typically hear of pushing people ashore or consorting (usually as individuals) with swimmers near the beach. Because they are not overly shy in the wild, the bottlenose dolphin can be followed and

Fraser's dolphins, a relatively new species, porpoising.

even trained in open water environments; in some cases, there are open pens, or lagoons, where dolphins can come and go, yet they allow themselves to be trained and willingly perform. It could be said that these individuals are 'feral' in that they have adapted to a quasi-urban environment.

The rough-toothed dolphin (*Steno bredanensis*), revealing its sloped head.

The other performing 'celebrity' of the dolphin world is the familiar, black-and-white orca, or killer whale, the males of which can reach 8 metres (32 ft) in length and can weigh close to 7,000 kilograms (8 short tons). The orca is one of the largest mammals ever to have existed, and is certainly the largest extant predatory mammal. To be sure, the size of the killer whale is an exception among dolphins, as is the fact that killer whales can be found in virtually all of the world's oceans and so, 'with the exception of humans, is the most wide-ranging mammal on earth'.[2]

The killer whale, *Orcinus orca*, is generally not thought of as a dolphin, yet despite its impressive size and its sometimes carnivorous diet, it is unequivocally a member of Delphinidae.

Nowadays, in fact, it is more fashionable to refer to the species simply as orcas, thereby eliminating the negative implications of 'killer' and setting aside the misleading term 'whale'. There is, of course, no mistaking the orca. In addition to its remarkable size, its uniquely stark black-and-white pattern includes a white oval patch over the eye and a white underbelly that covers the entire neck and radiates on either side of the urogenital area. A saddle of grey-white appears just behind the impressive dorsal fin, which in males can reach a height of 2 metres, and is boldly triangular. The orca's dramatic colour pattern may serve to visually break up its large form, thereby allowing it to approach prey more discreetly. The dorsal fin in females, though still impressive, is smaller and more falcate, but the flippers of both genders are extremely large and lobe-shaped, unlike those of any other dolphin.

Less common in tropical climes than in frigid waters, the orca is nevertheless found throughout the world. Orcas are very social and seem to be matriarchal, travelling in pods of up to 60 animals in which more than half of the animals are females and immature males. The remaining animals are equally divided between calves and mature males. Pregnancy lasts about fifteen to eighteen months, and there appears to be an interval of about five years between births.

In the waters near Washington state and British Columbia, where orcas have been studied intensely, a distinction is made between 'transient' groups, which are more likely to prey on seals, and 'resident' groups, which limit themselves exclusively to fish in general and salmon in particular. Oceanic orcas are more eclectic in their tastes and more likely to attack and eat larger whales, such as the minke and the gray. Whatever the prey, from fish corralled into bait balls (large clusters of schooling fish) to seals, whales and even the occasional moose tragically caught unawares while swimming a channel, orcas typically hunt cooperatively in groups and their hunting strategy has often been compared to that of wolves. Killer whales can be trained and have been kept in captivity in large aquaria, and are considered a major attraction because of their spectacular jumps and companionable behaviour. Still, any pool used for orcas is necessarily

A spinner dolphin (*Stenella longirostris*) leaping in a spiral.

Two orcas, showing the distinctive triangular dorsal fin of a male and the more curved fin of the female (foreground).

small and limiting, given their vast range in the wild, and there have been incidents where trainers have been attacked, or very infrequently killed, by captive whales. Orcas in captivity are often kept apart from other animals and have been known to mope; a telltale sign of an orca in captivity is a drooping dorsal fin.

FRESHWATER DOLPHINS

Although dolphins are generally considered marine mammals, about five species, primarily centred along the Amazon, Orinoco, Ganges, Brahmaputra and Yangtze rivers, actually live in fresh water. Adapted to river environments, these dolphins are not only smaller and more flexible than their marine relatives but they have longer (and perhaps more sensitive) beaks, in order to root around in sandy river bottoms. Furthermore, because rivers tend to have more sediment, the visual abilities of river dolphins is greatly reduced. The Amazon river dolphin, also called the bouto, boto or bufeo, is perhaps the best known of the river dolphins, if only because of its distinctive pink coloration. India,

Three bottlenose dolphins.

Bangladesh and Pakistan share what appears to be a common species, *Platanista gangetica*, which can be found in the Ganges, Indus and Brahmaputra rivers. Although widely distributed, these 'South Asia dolphins' are facing extinction because of pollution, poaching, damming projects and general encroachment of human populations. Muddy waters in rivers and intra-coastal waterways make for difficult observation, so the habits of species like the blunt-nosed Irrawaddy dolphin, that favours the brackish waters and estuaries near the mouths of the Ganges and Irrawaddy rivers, are still something of a mystery.

The movement of dolphins into river environments represents yet another remarkable adaptation for animals that had been predominantly marine, although the advantages of adapting to what was an unoccupied niche must have been compelling for ancient cetaceans.[3] Unfortunately, rivers inevitably attract human populations, which, particularly in the industrial era, led to the deterioration of river ecosystems. In recent years, the most notable victim of human encroachment and environmental deterioration was the baiji, or Yangtze river dolphin, which, having once ranged far along the Yangtze, was finally declared extinct in 2006.

The Irrawaddy dolphin or Orcaella.

The Amazon river
dolphin, which is
distinctly pink.

The evolutionary adaptation to rivers may be observed in
the tucuxi (*Sotalia fluviatilis*), a coastal oceanic dolphin with
riverine tendencies. Although the tucuxi is often grouped with
the freshwater dolphins, it is not actually believed be related to
them in any way. Their impressive adaptation to salt water and
brackish environments along the coast as well as fresh water in
the Amazon and Orinoco rivers remains a bit of a puzzle to cetologists. To be sure, the intersection of two different ecotopes,

The now extinct
Yangtze river
dolphin or Baiji.

such as the 'edge' between forest and field or salt and fresh water,
are known to be attractive zones for animals, which can benefit
from both prey and protection in the two different zones.

If an overview of the zoology and physiology of the many
species of dolphins tells us anything, it is that these animals have
had a very long evolutionary history. Over the last 35 million years,
dolphins have undergone radical anatomical and physiological
changes to adjust to the considerable demands of ocean life, and
have managed to inhabit almost every marine environment con-
ceivable. The fact that some species have even gone back to the
freshwater shallows and rivers that once harboured their ancestors is even more impressive when we consider the expansion
and radiation of dolphins worldwide. Like so many other aquatic
species, particularly those known as 'top carnivores', dolphins are
now threatened by pollutants, overfishing and human predation.
While the diversity precludes any single overarching response to

help protect them, it is also true that our attempts to gather data about individual species aid our appreciation of what actually constitutes a 'dolphin' and how we can apply that knowledge for the benefit of each surviving species.

3 The Dolphin in History and Mythology

Only to the Dolphin alone, beyond all other, nature has granted what the best philosophers seek: friendship for no advantage.
Plutarch (c. 46–c. 120 CE), *Moralia*

It is impossible to say when the first dolphin consented to swim with a human being, but Western tradition has conveniently given us the story of Arion, the ancient Greek poet-musician, as the first instance of human–dolphin interaction. Historically, dolphins were never truly domesticated and very rarely kept in captivity, yet the idea of the dolphin as a 'companionable' animal, comfortable with – if not actually connected to – humans is deeply embedded in myth and legend.

Despite the long history of the dolphin's relationship with humanity, very early depictions of dolphins are few indeed.[1] Prehistoric artefacts are rare, although a cave painting from Groote island in Northern Australia depicts a human and a dolphin together. The image probably traces the origin of human tribes as conceived in one of the Dreamtime legends of the Wanung-amulangwa people of Northern Australia. Like many other dolphin myths, the story of Dinginjabana, a reckless dolphin, not only establishes an intimate connection between man and dolphin but also captures in wonderful detail the essence of dolphin behaviour. The legend tells of the days in Dreamtime, the time before memory, when spirit beings appearing as animals inhabited the world. When they took the form of playful dolphins, these *indjebena* dolphin spirits, led by Dinginjabana, teased the sessile shellfish, the *yakuna*, for lacking grace and mobility. The

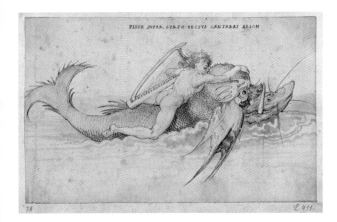

sole exception was Ganadja, the wife of Dinginjabana, who protested against the mistreatment of the *yakuna*. The *yakuna*, on the other hand, mocked the dolphins for mindless chatter: 'They talk all the time because they love the sound of their voices, not because they speak wisdom.'[2] Baringgwa, the leader of the *yakuna*, was particularly harsh towards the dolphins, and was finally dislodged from his spot and tossed around by Dinginjabana and his fellow dolphins, against considerable protest from Ganadja. When harassed by the dolphins, the *yakuna* typically cried 'Shark!' in an effort to scare the dolphins away, but the dolphins knew this trick too well to be fooled. Still, Baringgwa tried this ruse anyway and called out for the sharks who were, in fact, nearby. The sharks could not help but hear the uproar and savagely descended on all the dolphins except Ganadja, around whom the *yakuna* bound themselves, armouring her against attack. With Dinginjabana and all the other dolphins gone, Ganadja was inconsolable until she learned that her dolphin companions had dried up, having lost their spirit, and had taken human form on land. Ganadja was so desperate to pursue Dinginjabana that she beached herself

The Chumash Indians carved animal effigies, such as this killer whale, from stone. Their purpose is not well understood.

Sedna, having lost her fingers, is transformed into a sea creature.

and, seeing his human form, was herself transformed into a woman. Such were the beginnings of human tribes. The myth also provides an explanation for the perplexing tendency of dolphins to beach themselves: dolphins are often so desperate to find their former soulmates, they will beach themselves as Ganadja did, hoping for a positive outcome.

As in many folkloric traditions, the early animal myths based on dolphins explore the idea of shared identity across species. To that end, the characters in many are humans who have been transformed into dolphins, or dolphins that have adopted the human form. The Native American Chumash people for example, who live along the coast of California, have a legend originating on the island of Santa Cruz, which according to Native lore was becoming overpopulated. The goddess Hutash provided a rainbow bridge to allow many of the Chumash to move to the mainland, where they would settle in more open spaces. Alas, some who crossed the bridge fell into the water and might have drowned had not the compassionate Hutash transformed them into dolphins; thus dolphins are claimed by the Chumash as brethren. [3]

Not surprisingly, the Inuit have several myths that focus on marine mammals in general. One of the more frequently represented, in sculpture and prints, is the story of the beautiful maiden Sedna, who though widely pursued by suitors, finally chose to marry a dog.[4] Infuriated, Sedna's rejected suitors took her out to sea and cast her overboard. When she desperately grasped the boat, trying to climb back on board, the suitors chopped her fingers off, which, one by one, dropped into the sea, each becoming one of the great marine mammals of the North. Sedna herself became the goddess of the sea and, if displeased, frustrates the hunting of the Inuit people.

Among the Haida people living off the northwest coast of British Columbia, a story is told of a man stranded on a beach,

A stone axe, depicting a man attired with a dolphin, produced by the Totonac civilization possibly *c.* 900 from Veracruz-Liave, on Mexico's Gulf Coast.

who raised two small dogs. As they grew, they learned to swim out in the water to kill whales, which they brought back to land for their master. But they were far too successful and the meat that accumulated began to spoil. Displeased with their behaviour, the god created a fog on their next venture out to sea and, having lost their way back to land, were transformed into killer whales, which from that moment onwards were known as the 'wolves of the sea'.

The Ganges river dolphin (*Platanista gangetica*), a freshwater species, which is also called the susu, the blind river dolphin and

74

the side-swimming dolphin, has always had a mythical association with the Ganges river and was declared India's 'National
Aquatic Animal' in 2010.[5] Known as the Makara in Sanskrit, the
dolphin serves as a vehicle, or mount, for the goddess Ganga.
While some images represent the Makara as an elephant and others as a fish, many depictions of Ganga show her clearly atop a
dolphin (albeit with legs), complete with a typical river dolphin
rostrum (beak) filled with dozens of conical teeth. The elevation of
the Ganges dolphin to the status of National Aquatic Animal is a
distinction that in part reflects the fragility of freshwater cetaceans,
which suffer as a result of pollution and poaching.[6] Thus the
Ganges dolphin was also 'honoured' by a Conservation Action
Plan (2010–2020) to try to restore the approximately 2,000
remaining individuals to healthier numbers. A critical and chal-
lenging part of the plan is to improve water quality in the river
basins associated with both the Ganges and the Indus rivers.

Even though conservation efforts like those directed at the
Ganges river dolphin seem a little belated, we can only hope that
this movement and similar efforts will help species reach sus-
tainable populations. One of the most alarming recent events in
the world of conservation was the announcement in 2006 that
the baiji – the so-called Goddess of the Yangtze – is officially
extinct. A victim of the degraded condition of the river and of
human encroachment, the baiji, or Yangtze river dolphin (*Lipotes
vexillifer*), could not be saved.[7] Now all that remains of the
species is the wonderful legend told about its origins. The dolphin's name is believed to have derived from the daughter of Bai,
a ruthless father who harboured illicit desires for his daughter.
So intense was his ardour that he drowned her rather than see
her marry a young steward. The slain daughter was transformed
into a lovely white baiji, and the father was exiled. One version
of the legend has it that upon his voyage home, the unrepentant

and still predatory father raped a young woman on the boat. She committed suicide by throwing herself overboard, and cursed him for acting like a beast. In the ensuing storm, the father himself drowned and was transformed into the black finless porpoise (*Neophocaena phocaenoides*), a creature found in the waters of the Yangtze and derided as *jiangzhu*, or the 'river pig'.

The South American bouto (*Inia geoffrensis*), also called the Amazon river dolphin, pink river dolphin or the bufeo, is a freshwater dolphin that can still be found in relatively strong numbers in the river systems associated with the Orinoco, the Amazon and the Araguaia. Nevertheless, it is considered 'Vulnerable' by the International Union for the Conservation of Nature and Natural Resources (IUCN) as a consequence of industrial pollution, deforestation, abundant untreated sewage in the rivers, and poaching by non-natives who have settled in the region. The respect or perhaps fear that they have earned from surrounding peoples, who have historically considered the dolphins 'enchanted', has helped protect their numbers. All river dolphins, of course, live in much greater proximity to humans than their oceanic relatives, and thus some very strong relationships have resulted. But by the same token, as with the baiji and Ganges river dolphin, it also places these populations in much greater peril. Some of the qualities of the bouto may contribute to the positive attention it has received from neighbouring humans. Equipped with a remarkably flexible neck (in comparison to the rigid necks of most other species), a pinkish colour and a tendency to travel alone or in pairs, the bouto seems to have qualities that are particularly attractive to the human imagination.

The myth of Boto Encantado, or 'enchanted' dolphin, explains that some of these dolphins, often in the darkness of night, can transform themselves into humans and are motivated to seduce human women. They are said to appear during festivals when dances are held and they inevitably arrive dressed completely in white, wearing a hat that covers their blowhole, the telltale mark that cannot be disguised. In some versions of the legend, the dolphin lovers reveal themselves at the height of lovemaking and invite their partners to join the aquatic kingdom. But generally the dolphins disappear alone, returning to the water in the early morning having cast a spell on the young women so that they cannot recall the night of intimacy. But the story is far from over: months later the women who had been seduced find themselves pregnant. Some of these women are treated by local shamans, who administer abortion medications, while others give birth to their offspring; in the place on the register where the father's name is asked for, they write, simply, 'Dolphin'. Stories are also told of confrontations between a husband and the mysterious dolphin lover, whom he takes to be human. The following morning an actual dolphin appears with a knife embedded in its side, a martyr perhaps to the machismo of scorned or cuckolded lovers. If the legend strikes us as an elaborate ruse to justify an evening of illicit passion, it is nonetheless significant that a dolphin, of all creatures, serves as the figure of blame.

Less common, but still part of the same tradition, are the females – the Bota Encantada – who leave the water to seduce men. Some myths suggest that the boutos in general are shapeshifters (immortal in some traditions) who have simply opted to remain in dolphin form.[8] Other myths of humans being transformed into dolphins or vice versa are very common, though none have the widespread popularity of the selkie, the seal in Irish lore that sheds its skin and is transformed into a human, often living among them and having families while also longing for the sea.[9]

In general, dolphin myths cannot be distilled into a few narrow themes, but the frequent association between dolphins and

vulnerable young women is hard to ignore. It may well be that the graceful and slender shape of so many dolphin species evokes a sense of the feminine. Or perhaps societies found the fact that these aquatic creatures, which are lactating mammals like themselves, so arresting that the myths surrounding the creatures were themselves gendered female, as if to remind audiences and storytellers that dolphins and humans share a very primal connection.

Myths and legends in the early Western tradition reflect a fascination with dolphin–human rescues and dolphin vocalization. Interestingly enough, the early Egyptians – despite their proximity to the sea – seem to have had little interest in dolphins, and dolphins do not often appear in Egyptian mythology or artwork. The 'Dolphin Vase of Lisht', which dates to around 1750–1700 BCE during the Middle Kingdom, may be an exception to the rule, but even in style the dolphins resemble Minoan designs rather than anything that could be described as distinctly Egyptian.

The geographical setting for early Western culture, which emerged along the shores of the Mediterranean, the Adriatic and the Aegean, brought early civilizations into contact with dolphins on a regular basis. Living cheek by jowl, as it were, with dolphins, the early residents of the Mediterranean had many opportunities to observe dolphin behaviour, whether listening to them from a distance or sharing space with them in the shallows. Some of the earliest images of dolphins are from the Minoan Palace of Knossos in Crete, which was active from about 1700 to 1400 BCE. In these murals the dolphins are depicted in a natural setting without human riders or intervening gods. Similar images of dolphins as animals in the wild can be found in Greek and (much later) Roman mosaics and on coins, where the dolphins may not only have been decorative features but perhaps signified the maritime prowess of the Greek and Roman navies.

Pink dolphins in their enchanted state.

One of the oldest dolphin stories in Greek mythology is tied to the ancient temple of the Oracle at Delphi, which was originally believed to have been a temple dedicated to Gaia. The prevailing myth of the Oracle is that Apollo, having discovered the site of the Pythian Oracle at the base of Mount Parnassus, destroyed the snake that guarded it and claimed it for himself. Needing priests, Apollo took to the sea in the shape of a dolphin and guided a ship of unsuspecting sailors who were to become the priests at the oracular site we know as Delphi. Homer tells part of the story, from Apollo's perspective, in a hymn (translated here in prose):

> Apollo himself had a strong affinity for dolphins that emerged.
> And whereas I first, in the misty sea, sprang aboard the swift ship in the guise of a dolphin, therefore pray to me

A silver
dekadrachm
from Syracuse
(400 BCE).

as Apollo Delphinius, while mine shall ever be the Delphian altar seen from afar.[10]

Always the musician, Apollo (sometimes called Delphinios, Δελφίνιος, 'the Delphinian') like Arion was known for carrying a lyre with him and he more than occasionally accompanied himself while singing. Who better then, among the pantheon of Greek gods, to be represented by the image of the dolphin?

The origin of the word 'dolphin' is probably from *delphys*, the Greek word for womb, indicating an early awareness that this fish-like animal, contrary to what one might expect, has a womb and bears its young live. The connection between the animal and the presence of a womb may well have dictated the gender of the Delphic oracles, priestesses who, under the narcotic effects of a mysterious ether that we now believe to be ethylene, prophesied to visiting pilgrims.[11]

Aphrodite rising from the sea on the back of a dolphin.

The dolphin is often associated with Aphrodite, the goddess of love who rose from the sea. Her 'son', Eros (later Cupid in the Roman pantheon), is depicted even more frequently either holding or riding a dolphin.

Whether the many versions of the story of Arion the musician and the dolphin are derived from Apollo is unclear, but it stands to reason that Arion's status as a mortal is what makes his rescue by dolphins so compelling. As told by Herodotus (*c.* 484–*c.* 425 BCE), the great musician Arion had earned a substantial sum of gold performing throughout Sicily but longed to return to his native Corinth and hired a ship for that purpose.

But the sailors, attracted by Arion's considerable prize, threw him overboard and pocketed his money. Waiting in the sea, however, were dolphins who had heard him play an ode to Apollo on the lyre. So moved were they by Arion's music that they chose to rescue him and restore him to land. This myth, and others, repeats two dominant themes. First is an awareness

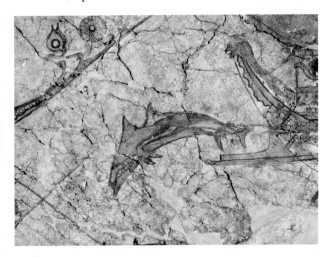

One of the earliest representations of dolphins in the wild: a dolphin frieze from the palace at Knossos c. 1,350 BCE.

A 13th-century BC Minoan wall painting of a ship's prow and dolphins from the island of Thera (Santorini).

A Roman mosaic (4th century AD) of cupids, dolphins and sealife from Utique on the northern coast of Tunisia.

of the dolphin's sensitivity to sound and perhaps even some understanding of the range of whistles ('music') the animals produce themselves. Aristophanes (*c.* 446–*c.* 386 BCE), for example, in his play *Frogs*, invoked the 'flute-loving dolphins that run / In the wake of the dark-blow slicing prows'.[12] Second is the belief in the dolphin's ability to appreciate the value of human life, which may be tied to an apparent understanding that humans are air breathers; they may even grasp that humans are terrestrial. Dolphin echolocation is sensitive enough to identify that humans, like themselves and like the newborn young they push to the surface for their first breath of air, have a large thoracic space to store air. In other words, that both species have lungs.

Arion's adventure, still the best-known myth about dolphins, has endured for a reason. In it we find allusions to some of the most compelling features of the dolphin, not least of which is the animal's seeming willingness to interact with humans. This is the earliest 'record' of a dolphin rescuing a human castaway, a narrative that has repeated itself through history all the way to the ordeal of Elián González, the son of Cuban refugees, who in 1999 claimed to have been rescued by dolphins while at sea.[13]

Ultimately, all of these rescue narratives afford the dolphin a sense of generosity and altruism that extends beyond its own species, to humans.

Arion's rescue is noteworthy because he was a mortal, but even the Greek gods themselves were clearly on good terms with dolphins. Poseidon, rejected by Amphitrite, relied on a dolphin as an emissary, not only to seek her out but to woo her as well. To reward the dolphin, Poseidon created the constellation Delphinus in its honour. Poseidon continued to use dolphins as messengers and they are often included in depictions of him. The god Dionysus, in the guise of a prince, was said to have been threatened by Etruscan pirates and, in order to frighten them, he turned the ship's oars, mast and rigging into snakes. So alarmed were the pirates that they all leaped into the sea, where they would have drowned, but in consequence of Dionysus' pity they were transformed into dolphins.

Classical Hellenic stories about dolphins shrewdly adapt the qualities of dolphin behaviour – including intelligence, insight and even humour – into their narratives. One of the most charming of Aesop's (c. 620–564 BCE) fables, for example, is the tale of a monkey rescued by a dolphin who mistakes it for a human being. 'Are you an Athenian?' the dolphin asks of the monkey, to which the monkey responds positively. 'Then you must know Piraeus', the dolphin enquires more suspiciously. 'Yes,' says the monkey, mistaking the port city of Athens for an actual person, 'I know him quite well; we are fast friends.' Then the dolphin, Aesop explains, drops the monkey from his back, allowing it to drown, and goes in search of real humans who need to be rescued. Aesop's allegiance to the intelligence and integrity of dolphins is clear; they are far too smart and resourceful to be hoodwinked by a mere monkey. The moral for us, according to Aesop, is: 'He who once begins to tell falsehoods is obliged to tell others to make them appear true, and, sooner or later, they will get him into trouble.'[14]

Notwithstanding the fact that dolphins were accepted as what we now call 'mammals' far back in the historical record, it is not difficult to understand why dolphins might have been mistaken for fish. But by the same token, enough was written and understood about dolphins to indicate that they were something other than the common fish. Aristotle (384–322 BCE), for example, was unequivocal in his *Historia animalium* about the fact that dolphins were mammals. His observations were not only meticulous in noting 'a blow-hole instead of gills' as well as lungs, but in recognizing that 'the dolphin and the porpoise are provided with milk, and suckle their young.' 'The creature', Aristotle details quite precisely, 'is remarkable for the strength of its parental affection.'[15]

The constellation 'Delphinus' depicted in Johannes Helvelius's *Firmamentum* (1687).

86

Plutarch (46–120 CE), born in a town around 30 kilometres
(20 miles) from Delphi, was no less enchanted by the dolphin,
describing it 'the only animal that would befriend humans for
no other reason than friendship'. In his *Lives*, Plutarch supports
his claim about dolphins with three stories. First is that of 'Enalus
the Aeolian', who threw himself into the sea to seek the same fate
as his lover, a virgin who was to be sacificed to Amphitrite and
the Nereids but both were saved by dolphins. Second is the story
of Jasus, who regularly swam and played with a dolphin that 'joy-
fully carried him which way soever the lad, by the motion of his
body, turned him'. Caught in a storm, Jasus was thrown from the
dolphin's back and drowned. The dolphin, Plutarch tells us:

took up the dead youth, and threw himself upon the land together with the body, from which he never stirred till he died out of his own element; deeming it but just to partake of that end of which he seemed to have been the occasion to his friend and playfellow.[16]

Finally, there is the story of Coeranus, who discovered several dolphins caught in a net and available for purchase in the local marketplace. According to legend, Coeranus bought the dolphins and released them back into the sea, only to be rescued by them when, on an ocean voyage, his boat was wrecked, killing all aboard. Coeranus, we are told, was saved by a dolphin that 'hastened to his rescue' and brought him to land. Nor does the story end there. When Coeranus died, his body was cremated near the ocean, where 'several dolphins appeared near the shore, as if they had come to his funeral; nor would they stir till the funeral was over'.

Whether Plutarch actually believed this touching story is beside the point; he was merely trying to evoke an impression shared by coastal dwelling peoples, that dolphins are intelligent, sensitive and have a special affinity for humans. No doubt sailors and fishermen had observed dolphins caring for their young, and perhaps even lingering over the bodies of recently deceased animals. Both behaviours are well documented among many species of dolphins, and the inclination to attribute similarities in parenting and mourning to both dolphins and humans is understandable.

Virtually all of the myths that involve dolphins are attempts to capture a sense of their sociability, intelligence and what seems to be a natural comfort with humans. In his poem on fishing, 'The Halieutica', the second-century CE poet Oppian (fl. 161–180) not only distinguishes dolphins from fish in general, he recognizes a special status for them based on the care they extend to their young and the friendship they seem to exude towards each other. Thus, writes Oppian – as paraphrased by the poet Alan Dugan, 'The hunting of dolphins is immoral',

> and the man who wilfully kills them
> will not only not go to the gods
> as a welcome sacrifice, or touch
> their altars with clean hands, but will
> even pollute the people under his own roof.[17]

That dolphins seem sociable and friendly among themselves is one thing, but some of these stories may exaggerate the level of goodwill they have towards humans. It should be noted that the 'friendliness' of dolphins towards humans is certainly species-specific, and even when observed, the exceptions (when dolphins and humans 'bond') should not be taken as the rule. Nevertheless, there are enough examples of cooperative hunting with humans and spontaneous interactions between wild dolphins and seaside bathers to suggest that humans have viewed the dolphin with respect and admiration for centuries. In recent decades, we might add 'awe' to the way that some humans regard dolphins; for them, the human–dolphin connection is a spiritual one (mystical in many cases) that transcends corporeal reality.

Although the dolphin is not frequently invoked in the contemporary Christian tradition, it has a long history as a Christian symbol of salvation, perhaps owing to the many stories of their rescuing the nearly drowned and restoring them to shore. The air-breathing dolphin, which disappears into impenetrable depths only to rise again, must have evoked a symbolic sense of resurrection and baptism for the early Christians whose lives also depended on the Mediterranean. Drawing on a Roman illustration (often

Terracotta hydria, or water vessel, from the 4th to 2nd centuries BCE, depicting a female figure and two dolphins from the Greek island of Hydra.

found on coins and in mosaics), the dolphin is frequently represented intertwined with an anchor, another symbol of salvation and, of course, the cross. The image is understood to combine the prudence, wisdom and agility of the dolphin – attributes that remind us to pursue the teachings of Christ swiftly – along with the solidity and utility of the anchor – encouraging us to bind ourselves to Christian principles. Associated with the proverb '*Festina lente*' ('hasten, slowly'), the symbol – now called the Aldine Pickering Anchor – was taken up by the great Renaissance publisher, Aldus Manutius, and later in the nineteenth century by the English publisher William Pickering.

Interest in the dolphin, whether as a symbol or an actual animal, seems to have waned throughout the early Christian and Byzantine eras. As cultures moved away from isolation and introspection, however, interest in the animal world was revived, and some degree of curiosity about dolphins was renewed. Medieval authorities on dolphins were often quirky in their knowledge of the animals, but obviously drew on some first-hand knowledge or upon informed reports from mariners. Bartholomaeus Anglicus (c. 1203–1272), the medieval Franciscan scholar, appreciated the fact that dolphins might actually rescue humans at sea but offers a peculiar caveat, noting that 'when a man is drowning, dolphins can tell from the odor whether he has ever eaten the flesh of a dolphin. If he has not, they rescue him and bring him safe to land; if he has, they devour him on the spot.'[18] The level of protection said to be offered by dolphins was extensive; Bartholomaeus notes that a dolphin 'keepeth and defendeth him [a human] from eating and biting of other fish, and shoveth him, and bringeth him to the cliff with his own working.'[19]

In the medieval bestiary 'The Book of Beasts', the entry on dolphins not only notes (anticipating the *Flipper* theme song) that 'nothing in the sea is faster than they are' but focuses on the auditory capacities of the dolphin: 'They follow the human voice', the author explains, and 'will assemble together in schools for a symphony concert'.[20] Despite these insightful observations, the author enters the realm of the fantastic by remarking: 'there is a species of Dolphin in the River Nile, with a saw-shaped dorsal fin, which destroys crocodiles by slicing up the soft parts of the belly.' Yet the fantasy persisted, and more than a few illustrations of dolphins from the period depict the dorsal fin as serrated.

Notwithstanding spurious anatomical features, the question of how to classify the dolphin – from a zoological perspective – remained confusing to many naturalists. Peter the Spaniard, known as Petrus Hispanus, a Portuguese physician (who may also have been Pope John xxi, elected in 1276), was understandably stymied by cetacean biology and posed the following question: 'Why [do] the dolphin and whale have true blood, albeit they are fish?'[21] The confusion or conflation of fish and dolphins is reflected in the heraldic Dacre Dolphin, one of four 'Dacre Beasts' commissioned by Lord Thomas Dacre of Naworth Castle, Cumbria, prior to 1520. Although it is clearly scaled like a fish, it is meant to reflect the family arms of the Greystokes, Lady Dacre's family; the creature wears a crown that signifies the ascendancy of dolphins over all marine mammals. Indeed, cetaceans were confusing to many early naturalists, who often relied on the habitat of an animal to determine its taxonomic status; in short, it was as difficult to conceive of a mammal in water as it was to consider a fish out of water.

Local knowledge about dolphins was not always documented, but many communities had long-standing relationships with dolphins, whose stories then became part of regional lore. In what might be considered an unlikely turn of events, it was the experience of a local culture that resulted in the application of the term 'le Dauphin' to the heir to the French throne. The term is derived from the Dauphiné, an area on the Mediterranean in southern France, which had been an independent state under the rule of the Counts of Albon and Vienne. Citizens of the region had come to be known as *dauphinois*, and the escutcheon of the territory bore the image of a dolphin. When Humbert ii, the final Count of Albon and Vienne, incurred an insurmountable debt in 1349, he ceded the region to Charles of Valois (1338–1380), later Charles v, stipulating that the future heirs to the throne of France

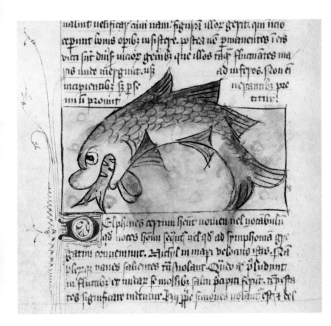

A dolphin with a 'serrated' back, from the 'Bestiary of Anne Walsh' (1633).

would be known as 'le Dauphin', just as the heir to the British throne is known as the Prince of Wales. From that time forwards, until the French Revolution, the designation 'le Dauphin' (complete with dolphins as an emblem) remained the title of the successor to the French throne. Sir Walter Scott's Waverley novels revived interest in the fate of the Dauphin after the revolution, and this interest extended as far as Mark Twain's Huck Finn, who anglicizes the name as he tells Jim about the misadventures of 'the dolphin' of France.[22]

While dolphins were a common sight for many Europeans, killer whales were probably spotted only infrequently. The great early modern naturalist Konrad Gesner apparently observed – or at least learned of – a stranded killer whale on 30 March 1545, in the Greifswalder Bodden, a bay on Germany's Baltic coast. The

The arms of the Dauphin of France.

93

Konrad Gesner's killer whale in *Historiae animalium* (1551–8).

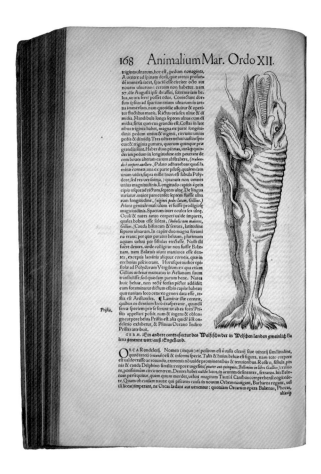

depiction of the whale in his *Historiae animalium* (1551–8) preserves the ferocious look of the whale, even to the point of enhancing the flippers to create claws, but dismisses less salient features, including the prominent dorsal fin. Elsewhere, however, Gesner includes the dorsal fin, in an image of killer whales (showing two blowholes rather than one) attacking a larger whale

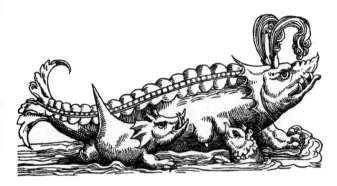

which, despite the fact that it was surely a baleen whale, also
has prominent teeth. But the whale under attack is rendered distinctly mammalian, as it is also suckling its young from a pair
of side-mounted teats.

Pierre Belon (1517–1564) includes dolphins in *L'histoire naturelle
des estranges poissons marins* (*The Natural History of Unusual Sea
Fishes*, 1551), yet he provides an illustration of a dolphin foetus
attached to the mother by an umbilicus and surrounded by a
placenta (as does Gesner in his natural history). We should not
be too surprised by the conflation of fish and dolphin characteristics, given the extent to which the confusion persists even
to the present day. The popularity of the illustrations found in
Belon and Gesner is attested to by Adriaen Coenen's 'Whale
Book', an illustrated manuscript from the sixteenth century. An
amateur naturalist, Coenen had a good eye for the cetaceans he
observed himself, but he also relied on established texts for his
own drawings.

Biological interest in dolphins waned once again through
the Renaissance to the mid-eighteenth century. Within the
decorative arts and visual culture, however, the image of the
dolphin proved very useful and popular, particularly in the

Dit is dat FAETSOE VAN DEN hil

'This is an illustration of the fish called a hil', from 'The Whale Book', an illustrated manuscript (*c.* 1585) by a Dutch amateur naturalist, Adriaen Coenen.

prolific representations of putti (young cherubic boys) with dolphins. Paintings drawing on classical themes such as Arion and Neptune abounded and the incorporation of dolphins in paintings or as ornamental elements in furniture, vases and murals became quite common through to the eighteenth century. Dolphins became a device, adding classical and mythic dimensions to the work of a new generation of artists less interested in natural history than aesthetics and classicism. But as an icon, whether of sexuality (in the arms of putti), friendship (in depictions of Arion) or elegance (in the finial elements of decorative objects), the dolphin form endured as a durable stock image. The architect Michael Graves has sustained that legacy by using the classical image of a dolphin as a massive decorative element at the Walt Disney World Dolphin Resort (constructed in 1990).

One of the early writers to codify the iconography of the dolphin was the Italian amateur scholar Cesare Ripa (1560–1622), whose dictionary of emblems, *Iconologia* (1593), became the standard European sourcebook of Christian emblems for centuries to come. Ripa reads the stock image of a child riding a dolphin as an emblem for 'A Gentle Disposition', supporting his observation with the dolphin's actual behavioural traits:

> A Child mounted on a Dolphin is a true Emblem of an affable courteous Disposition; because the Dolphin loves and caresses a Man out of *meer Instinct*, rather than Interest of sinister Design; as several ancient Histories inform us.[23]

Ripa also notes that the image of a dolphin with a bridle represents 'saving from danger', or *Salvezza*, which encompasses both the Christian ethos of salvation and the behavioural observations of dolphin rescues. Dolphins appear much less frequently in the Jewish tradition, but the Talmud (Bechoroth 8a) draws on the Rabbi Judah's pithy question: 'What are dolphins?' The answer is bold and straightforward: 'Humans of the sea.' The Talmud adds the more enigmatic (and perplexing) observation

Mother, placenta and foetus which was depicted in Pierre Belon's *Natural History* and in Gesner's *Historiae animalium.*

Ornamental
dolphins
supporting
an early
19th-century
fountain.

that 'Dolphins are fruitful and multiply by coupling with human beings.' Whether this simply suggests cooperating with humans, or some ancient and forgotten folklore that dolphins are actually half-human, half-animal, is unclear and probably, in the Talmudic spirit, irresolvable.

One of the seminal works that diverted attention away from the dolphin as emblem to the dolphin as organism was Edward Tyson's (1651–1708) *Phocaena; or, The Anatomy of a Porpess*, which was published in 1680. A physician and anatomist whose later

Michael Graves's monumental dolphin ornament for Disney.

works included a treatise on the orang-utan, Tyson was following a new trend in zoology that emphasized detailed accounts of the biology and anatomy of every species under consideration.

Perhaps influenced by Tyson's work, the British naturalist John Ray (1627–1725) made a break with precedent by classifying 'Cetae' (cetaceans) within the class Mammalia in his *Synopsis methodical animalium quadrupedum et serpentini generis* (1693). Carl Linnaeus (1707–1778), the ostensible 'father' of biological classification, was slow to follow suit. In his first edition of *Systema naturae* (1738), he reversed Ray's finding and classified whales, dolphins and porpoises with fish, but by the tenth edition (1758) he saw fit to restore them to the mammals.

From that time onwards, little doubt remained that dolphins were mammals and as travel and exploration increased, information about new species of dolphins was collected by sailors, amateur naturalists and whalers. Zoology, then 'natural philosophy', as a discipline was on the rise in France, and the movement witnessed an effort to make sense of the natural world as a rational system. At the lead was the Comte de Buffon (1707–1788), whose astonishing energy resulted in the 36 volumes of his *Histoire naturelle* (1749–88). Sustained by Jean-Baptiste Lamarck (1744–1829) and Georges Cuvier (1769–1832), zoology was emerging as a pragmatic and systematic discipline focused on the thorough analysis of each animal. Buffon's energy for zoological inquiry seems to have been contagious and his work was continued by his equally inexhaustible protégé, Bernard Germain de Lacépède (1756–1825). Among his many books was *Histoire*

'A Gentle Disposition', from Cesare Ripa's *Iconologia* (1593).

Cuvier's depiction of the Southern right whale dolphin.

des cétacés (1804), one of the first modern works devoted exclusively to whales and dolphins. At the same time, the great Cuvier, comparative anatomist par excellence, was classifying specimens received from fellow natural philosophers, who sought his help to resolve their discoveries. Thus Cuvier's name is attached to a variety of animals that he described for the literature; these included an odd variety of cetaceans, including Risso's dolphin (*Grampus griseus*, Cuvier 1812), Cuvier's beaked whale (*Ziphius cavirostris*, Cuvier, 1823) and the spotted dolphin (*Stenella frontalis*, Cuvier 1829).

While scientists like Cuvier were somewhat sedentary, other researchers were travelling the world on voyages of discovery. Darwin's six-year voyage, as we have seen, not only included his findings on the Galapagos Island, but also led to his identification of the dusky dolphin. Alexander von Humboldt (1769–1859) was an even more intrepid traveller whose extensive travels in South America were described in the monumental *Le voyage aux régions equinoxiales du Nouveau Continent, fait en 1799–1804* (1807). Humboldt extended the range of *Inia geoffrensis* (the Amazon river dolphin) to the distant and unconnected Orinoco river, which led to interesting questions – still unanswered – about where the species originated and how it migrated.

Dolphins attracted mostly academic interest throughout much of the nineteenth century, although attempts were made in the

Dauphin de Risso.

Risso's dolphin.

1860s to put cetaceans on display in aquaria. The first animals to be shown were beluga whales, captured in the St Lawrence and shipped by P. T. Barnum to his museum in New York, where they promptly died when housed in a freshwater tank.[24] The animals lived slightly longer in saltwater tanks, which were subsequently used by Barnum who recognized that even under those conditions, his display would not last long. 'This is probably the last attempt', Barnum wrote to his prospective customers, 'that will be made to exhibit a living whale in connection with the other expensive attractions of the Museum for only twenty-five cents.'[25] Other attempts were made by Barnum at the Aquarial Gardens of Boston and by others at London's Westminster Aquarium, but to no avail. In 1913 an effort was made by the American Museum of Natural History in New York to maintain five bottlenose dolphins, but within two years all of them were dead.[26] It was not until 1938 that an unlikely consortium, including W. Douglas Burden (a trustee of the American Museum of Natural History), Cornelius Vanderbilt Whitney, Sherman Pratt (of Standard Oil) and Ilia Tolstoy (grandson of Leo), founded Marine

Studios in St Augustine, Florida. It was the first time that a dolphin was kept – with relative success – in captivity. The solitary bottle-nose that inhabited the aquarium was a surprisingly popular attraction, drawing 20,000 tourists on opening day to a facility intended merely for filming marine life.[27]

The advent of captivity was a double-edged sword for the dolphin. On the one hand, having animals in aquaria enabled extremely detailed research about their behaviour and physiology, much of which is the foundation for all current research, whether in captivity or in the wild. On the other hand, however, it created a market for aquaria around the world, developed with the sole purpose of putting performing animals on display.

Despite the degree to which our understanding of dolphins has benefited from science, current popular perceptions of dolphins still owe a great deal to 'myth' in its broadest sense. These myths are so familiar that they have almost become embedded as commonplace beliefs, if not knowledge. Foremost among these beliefs is that all dolphins are like Flipper, ready to cast off life in the wild to buddy up with a human, or that dolphins are on the cusp of speaking to us with a shared vocabulary, or even that they embody a natural spiritualism to which humans can only aspire. These well-worn stories may well seem naïve or merely misguided, but they persist to such an extent that they have credence in contemporary culture. These are, in a sense, the new dolphin myths, which have contorted and adapted themes from the past to suit a modern culture that still sees dolphins as mysterious.

4 Intelligence, Social Behaviour and Echolocation

> I should like to hear a thoughtful and brilliant dolphin cutting us down to our true size, in that far day when the much-vaunted Dignity of Man becomes a footnote to history.
> James Thurber, 'Here Come the Dolphins', in *Lanterns and Lances* (1962)

As compelling as the idea of 'intelligence' may be, the cognitive and social abilities of dolphins need to be understood in their environmental context. Although we know dolphins very well from captivity, their natural home is in 'the wild', which can mean something very different as we shift from species to species. In short, while similarities across species – such as a marine habitat – allow for certain generalities, students of dolphin behaviour need to be alert to the subtle variations that exist among dolphin species and even particular dolphin communities.

Many dolphins have 'home ranges', or territories. In other words, they will only travel a certain distance within that range and will remain in that general area even as they move around to find food and shelter. The travelling that these dolphins undertake should not be mistaken for migration, which entails much more distant movements in order to pursue food or to return to breeding waters. When salmon move upstream in order to breed, killer whales in the Pacific Northwest must travel considerable distances to find other food sources. The movements of oceanic dolphins, such as Heaviside's dolphin and Commerson's dolphin, are attributable to various oceanographic features – currents and weather patterns for example – that also dictate the presence and availability of prey. The ocean is far from homogeneous and even seemingly close regions can differ noticeably – at least to dolphins – in terms of temperature, salinity, the effects of depth and other features, which ultimately determine the distribution of species that forage and reside in those areas. These differences contribute to the separation of species, and because oceanographic changes are also seasonal, the movements of these groups will vary with the time of year.

Dolphin pods can vary in number from small aggregates of fifteen animals to very large groups of up to 600 animals. But even within these very large groups, smaller pods will frequently break away for substantial periods of time. This represents a social structure in animal behaviour that has come to be known as fission-fusion. Thus while there may be an advantage for animals to congregate in large groups (for example, for safety), that community is actually composed of smaller stage groups that may forage together and serve as a kind of family unit.

Feeding is no less important for dolphins than for any other animal, and perhaps even more so, given that some species need to consume close to 8 per cent of their body weight on a daily basis. For a modestly sized bottlenose dolphin, that may mean up to 32 lbs of fish per day. Thus it makes sense that many dolphins work cooperatively while feeding, particularly when trying to capture schooling fish. A group of dolphins will frequently approach a large school of fish from various sides, and in doing so force the school into very tight formations called 'bait balls'. Individual dolphins then take turns diving through the bait ball in order to feed. In an almost counter-intuitive feeding strategy, termed 'strand feeding', dolphins off the coastal waters of the Carolinas will scare fish up onto the strand and follow them, as if beaching themselves. After eating several of the thrashing fish, the dolphins themselves must wriggle their way back into the water. Sounds produced by dolphins can stun fish, making them easier to capture; the same effect is often achieved by impressive

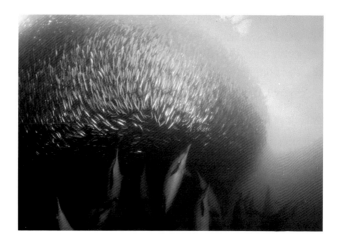

tail slaps, which leave fish dazed and therefore more accessible. In more open waters, dolphins will pursue squid and fish on an individual basis.

Play behaviour in dolphins can be extensive, and sexual play is very frequently incorporated into play activities. Young dolphins practise hunting skills and swimming manoeuvres, both to hone their skills and in an effort to determine social hierarchies. The remarkable synchrony of movements that are inevitably part of performances in oceanaria are part of their natural repertoire of skills. The advantages of synchronous movements are beginning to be examined, and it is clear that they may play a strong role in social bonding. The ability to move or act in unison is not merely instinctive (as it may be in animals that flock or school in large numbers), but can be coordinated between individuals. Dolphins have not only been trained, by Louis Herman and others, to invent new performative behaviours (such as innovative jumps), but to execute them in synchrony. Both tasks reflect very high cognitive abilities and, of course, sophisticated levels of communication and exchange. If synchronized movements can be so well coordinated, they may also have some advantage in serving as a distraction to either predators or prey, confusing them by suddenly presenting two separate forms when there had appeared only to be one.

While what appears to be sexual play is very common among dolphins, the actual act of copulation is very brief. That sexual play can keep several dolphins occupied for considerable amounts of time suggests that sex has a pleasurable aspect for dolphins as it does for humans. To accurately assess whether 'pleasure' is a motivating factor in sex is difficult (even in humans). What is clear is that dolphins are playful and will often touch or stroke each other around the urogenital region with

The Atlantic spotted dolphin mating with a younger and less spotted male.

their flippers, their beaks, their flukes and even their dorsal fins. This is not to say that copulation and sexual activity are always idyllic; pairs of younger males have been known to herd a female away from the pod and repeatedly attempt sexual intercourse in a way that appears to be forced rather than consensual.

Bottlenose dolphins are spontaneous ovulators, so there is no particular time for peak fertility, or oestrus, among females, though most calving is observed in the spring and autumn. There is a fair amount of variation with respect to sexual maturity in different species of dolphins. Killer whales, for example, do not appear to reach sexual maturity until they are fourteen years old, although males may be slightly more precocious. Maturity, that is, the age of reproductive ability, hovers around the ten-year-old mark for most species, although the common dolphin matures around two or three years old. Trying to identify sexual activity in dolphins is a bit more deceptive than in other animals. Males, for example, are capable of erection at will, which allows male dolphins to use an erect penis in unconventional ways, for example when retrieving a hoop or other objects. Unlike most mammals, including all primates except for humans, dolphins do not have a baculum (penis bone or *os penis*), although it is no more apparent why it should have disappeared in dolphins than why it vanished in human evolution. In females, it is unclear whether a post-copulatory 'vaginal plug' develops, as it does in some mammals, in order to retain semen after copulation has taken place. Although this would be an adaptation well suited to the aquatic environment, the plug may be precluded by a series of vaginal folds or valves that may actually funnel sperm towards the cervix, and no doubt also restrict any inward flow of seawater.

Dolphins are born after a gestational period of at least ten to twelve months and emerge tail first, in the position that is referred to among humans as a breech birth. The danger in humans is clear, given that the optimal presentation is to have the baby's head emerge first to capture that first breath of air. In dolphins, however, the infant emerges into a watery environment, which might lead to complications such as drowning, were the birth to be difficult or prolonged for some reason. There is very little data about the mortality rate of dolphins in the wild, but when a baby dolphin is stillborn, the attachment of the mother is remarkable. A dead newborn may be pushed along by its mother for weeks and possibly even months, until the 'infant' has decomposed beyond recognition and may look like nothing more than a small rag.

Elder females, or aunts, often attend the birthing process and may assist the mother or young in the birthing or 'nursery' area. What's more, their care-giving role will continue for several years as the dolphin calf matures into an adult. Although the young may start consuming fish after several months, a young dolphin will continue to nurse for up to two years, until it eventually participates in full-scale foraging and predatory behaviour. While it is difficult to determine how frequently dolphins suckle in the wild, young animals probably nurse a few times each hour in the early months of development. The maturation process is gradual and dolphin calves may remain with the mother for up to six years. As with other mammals, including artiodactyl (deer-like) relatives, males will frequently pair off and travel independently of the pod, eventually joining another pod.

ECHOLOCATION

One of the greatest challenges posed by diving into the very dense medium of water is the reduction of visibility. Dolphins have responded by developing a sophisticated system of echolocation, now often called biosonar, which allows the animals to navigate by use of sound. The notion that animals might be able to negotiate dark spaces using sound dates back to Lazzaro Spallanzani (1729–1799), who discovered that bats flew unimpeded when blindfolded, but were stymied in flight when their ears were plugged up. Spallanzani's findings were ridiculed by most of his colleagues and successors, including Cuvier, who believed that bats manoeuvred by the sense of touch. It was not until the mid-twentieth century that the zoologist Donald Griffin noticed that bats produced ultrasonic emissions, which ultimately led to his discovery of sonar in bats.

Even as Griffin was about to publish *Listening in the Dark* (1958), his groundbreaking study of echolocation in bats,[1] Arthur McBride, the curator of Marine Studios (later given the oxymoronic name, Marineland), had established that dolphins could avoid very fine nets underwater. A succession of researchers at Marineland, including William Schevill and Winthrop Kellogg, began to detail the production of sound by dolphins and to suggest that they too navigated by echolocation. Kellogg, the author of *Porpoises and Sonar*, found that dolphins could hear very high frequencies (120 kHz) and could distinguish between different species of fish presented simultaneously.[2] But it was Kenneth Norris, one of the founders of modern dolphin research, who provided conclusive evidence of echolocation in dolphins when he applied suction cup blindfolds to a dolphin, which subsequently navigated an underwater maze with no difficulty.[3] Norris, and other researchers, noted that sounds seemed to emanate from the melon of the dolphin, a bulbous fatty deposit in what is commonly taken to be its forehead. When objects drifted below the apparent scanning range of the melon, they could no longer be retrieved, thus establishing what might be called, for lack of better terminology, a field of auditory view. Norris also speculated that sounds were picked up and transmitted to the ear by the

Jumping Porpoises at Feeding Time
Marine Studios, Marineland, Fla.

MARINE
STUDIOS

An early publicity drawing from Marineland.

dolphin's lower jaw, an observation that has been corroborated and analysed in more recent research.

Human systems of echolocation date back to the early twentieth century, but the term SONAR (SOund NAvigation and Ranging) was coined during the Second World War as the military perfected it to target submarines. Echolocation in dolphins is a system by which animals emit sound waves that rebound off a 'target' object (such as a fish) in a pattern that is recognizable and decipherable to the animal. Most dolphins are capable of generating very high-frequency waves (at least 120,000 Hz), which because of their narrow wavelength can generate what we must assume are fairly precise images. Humans can hear up to 16,000 Hz (or cycles per second), which is less than one tenth of some of the sounds produced by dolphins. To employ the term 'images', however, is misleading, because it is not clear how the dolphins actually process the returning echoes. In medical sonograms, such as for pregnancy, the echoes reflecting off the foetus (or an organ) are translated into an image better suited to visually oriented humans. Typically, lower frequencies are used to generate these images, since high frequencies (with intense, rapid pulses per each millisecond) might damage the foetus. In fact, dolphins can actually employ their high-frequency sonar to stun schools of fish, which makes for less frantic chases and more convenient meals.

Although humans have very good hearing and rely heavily on sound to identify and even locate objects, it is still difficult to comprehend the refined use of sound in dolphins. A dolphin, whether swimming during the day or the evening, must always contend with limited light, water turbidity and murky conditions. Under all of these conditions, echolocation is used to penetrate and to 'read' through the water, observing (as it were) what is ahead of the animal and to determine, if necessary, the topography of the sea floor. Recent work by Whitlow Au has demonstrated that dolphins can detect, via echolocation, very small objects from a great distance and distinguish the density of objects presented to them. It is not surprising, then, that dolphins are excellent foragers of prey species that seek refuge under the sand (fish and crabs); although they disappear from sight, their form, shape and density are readily apparent to an echolocating dolphin. Even squid, whose bodies are roughly the density of water, betray themselves by having a dense beak at their core that, we must assume, can be detected from a substantial distance.

Dolphins may also have the ability to retain sonic images of each other, given that they have the capability to 'read' muscle from bone, an empty stomach from a full one and a pregnant uterus from a 'normal' or vacant one. All of this is enhanced by the fact that dolphins swim in water, which because of its density is an ideal medium for the transfer of sound waves. Bats, which also echolocate, face the additional obstacle of emitting sound in the air, which is a far less conductive medium for the transmission of sound.

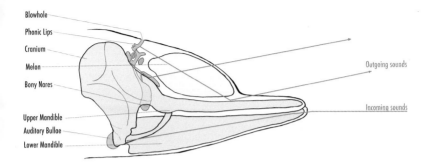

Blowhole
Phonic Lips
Cranium
Melon
Bony Nares
Upper Mandible
Auditory Bullae
Lower Mandible

Outgoing sounds
Incoming sounds

A cross-section of a dolphin's skull showing how sounds are produced and received.

Large whales can produce very low-frequency sounds (as elephants also do), which because of their broad wavelength can travel long distances. The simple way of thinking about this is that low-frequency waves when emitted are less frequent per second, and there is a great amount of energy carried by each wave. High-frequency sound waves, by contrast, are produced in very rapid succession, allowing for a more precise echo or image. But with less energy per wave, both the initial sound and the echo dissipate more quickly and are thus used over much shorter distances. The extent to which dolphins actually use low-frequency sounds (to communicate with other pods or stray individuals) is not clear, but they are nowhere as frequent in small whales and dolphins as they are in the 'great whales', which also migrate thousands of miles.

The sounds that we typically associate with echolocation are the rapid clicks that one can often hear when in the water with dolphins, or occasionally when pressing one's ear to the glass wall of an oceanarium. Needless to say, there is a broad range of sounds that we do not actually hear because they are well beyond our auditory range. Those sounds are rich with information for other dolphins, mediating environmental data and specific details about each animal or the group. It is not entirely clear how

Gesner's depiction
of a dolphin skull
and a foetus in
utero.

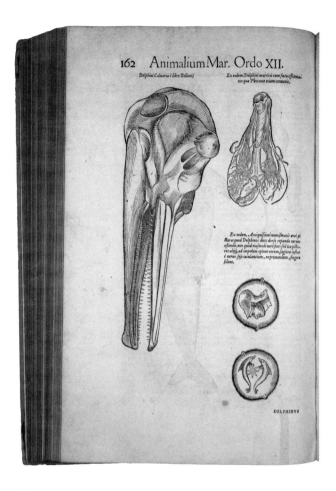

dolphins produce the very diverse sounds that they generate. Dolphins typically have a larynx (voicebox) out of which some sounds may be generated; but they also have a complicated system of air sacs (not to be confused with sinuses) in the nares, the nasal passages, that in dolphins come together to form a single nostril or 'blowhole' (other whales, the mysticetes, have two blow-holes). The sacs form what are called 'phonic lips' (previously called 'monkey lips') that seem capable of generating a variety of sounds, some of which are released as whistles through the blow-hole and some of which are contained within the nasal system of the dolphin and emitted as echolocation signals. Exactly how the emissions occur still perplexes scientists. But sounds are pro-pelled forwards, perhaps assisted by the parabolic shape of the dolphin's skull, and certainly modified by the 'lens' of fatty tissue called the melon. The melon, which appears to be the dolphin's forehead, actually sits in front of the blowhole and on top of the rostrum. The signal emitted by a dolphin is relatively limited in direction, emanating from the melon and extending upwards and to either side; the dolphin moves its head downwards to echolo-cate objects below its body.

No less perplexing than the production of sound is how exactly it is received. Dolphins do have two external openings on either side of their heads for the ear canals, although external ears were lost for the sake of streamlining, but these canals (upon which we as humans rely for sound) are blocked. Hear-ing in the dolphin, as Kenneth Norris proposed, takes place through the lower jaw of the animals, which captures sound and transmits it backwards to the tympana, which are associated with the lower jaw. The jaw contains fatty deposits that facili-tate the transmission of sound, and the inner ears are surrounded by muscle and fat in order to exclude sounds from other sources. A human swimming underwater is bombarded by sounds, most of which cannot be located. This is because we have no insulation of our inner ears, and so sounds are picked up by every part of the head and transferred simultaneously to our ears. The head of the dolphin is, by contrast, well insulated and so sounds travelling through the jaw are picked up by each ear individually. This kind of stereophonic effect allows the dolphin to triangulate the echoes it receives and pinpoint the source of the sound.

There is some speculation that dolphins may be able to 'eavesdrop' on the echoes produced by a fellow dolphin and thus, in a sense, 'read' the same information generated by the other dolphin without having to produce a signal on its own.[4] There are good reasons for thinking this might work, not least of which is efficiency. One signal will draw less attention to a group of dolphins than several, whether when searching for food or avoiding predators. But the complexity of auditory signalling makes this theory highly speculative.[5]

Among the most distinctive sounds produced by dolphins are the many whistles it produces both above and below the water's surface. Researchers have determined that all dolphins have what is called a 'signature' whistle that is unique to a single individual. These whistles, according to Vincent Janik, are relatively similar to names. In the wild, where visibility and distance can split groups up, it is advantageous, Janik argues, to be able to account specifically for all of the group members and unique tags (or names) would make that simpler.[6] Dolphins are wonderful mimics as well and can 'sound-match' each other's whistles, to say nothing of other sounds. It was this that prompted John Cunningham Lilly, as we shall see, to train dolphins to vocalize human words and possibly mimic human speech. But whistles are clearly not 'words' – they undoubtedly compress a great deal of information into forms that carry meaning, but in modes that are unfamiliar to us.

The desire to have dolphins speak to us, preferably in a language we understand, may go back millennia, but has really been a phenomenon of the late twentieth century. Language is, without doubt, the greatest indicator of intelligence but studies, such as those by John Cunningham Lilly, imposed on dolphins a pre-conceived concept of language that failed to take into account the animals' zoological and environmental constraints. As for defining 'intelligence', we know how difficult it is to define the word, whether in humans or other animals. If animal studies have shown us anything, it is that 'intelligence' must be measured qualitatively no less than quantitatively. Dogs, for example, seem foolish when they strain at a leash to pursue a squirrel up a tree. And squirrels, which are remarkably adept at running and jumping through the treetops, seem painfully limited and uninteresting as potential companion pets. Every animal, humans included, experiences the world around it through a unique array of sensory abilities. Not even the best scuba diver can appreciate what it is like to unerringly navigate the dense medium of water, as echolocating dolphins do. Nor are we attuned to the variety of tastes that may be mediated through the water, and we do not seem capable of sensing any kind of magnetic cues in the way that dolphins do.

The post-war years saw increased interest in physical psychology and neurology, which led to dramatic new findings about the human brain. It is hardly surprising that interest also turned to dolphins, which were known to have one of the largest brains – as calculated against body size – among mammals. Dolphin brains show the kind of complex convolutions (infolding) that are characteristic of human brains and which are assumed a primary indicator of complex cognitive abilities. The hypothesis then and now is that a brain so large has to be capable of remarkable feats of intelligence, if not intellect. That the cetacean brain had adapted to deal with an incredibly complex and sophisticated amount of information, necessitated by movement in a three-dimensional medium which apparently required the innovation of echolocation, was not necessarily at the fore of the minds of many researchers.[7] Large brains were thought to mean large capacity and, to some people's way of thinking, large ideas, while the social nature of dolphins and their active use of vocalizations underscored the notion that these were 'precocious' creatures. This is not to say that any of this is not true, but what it did lead to, for a decade or two at least, was a fascination among the public with the prospect of talking dolphins.

The move in this direction was led primarily by John Cunningham Lilly (1915–2001), a neuroscientist whose background in physics, medicine and computing led to an interest in the capacity of the brain for intelligence and language. After studying physics and biology at CalTech, Lilly received a medical degree from the University of Pennsylvania, where he also pursued biophysics and psychoanalysis. His early work during the Second World War and subsequently at the National Institute of Mental Health focused on the idea of the self as a constituted brain. To that end, he developed the 'isolation tank', a saltwater chamber where individuals, including Lilly and some of his colleagues, would float for hours at a time, divorced from virtually all potential stimulation to the brain. To monitor brain activity in animals, he developed ostensibly painless methods for inserting electrodes into the cortex, which could then be displayed on a monitor.

Lilly was attracted to research with dolphins because of their large brains and their ability to vocalize and mimic sounds presented to them. Convinced that human–dolphin communication

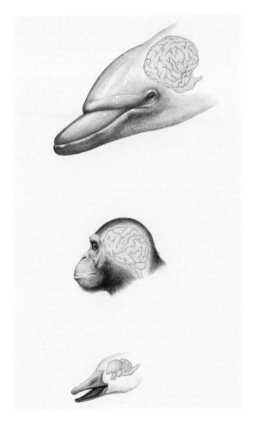

The large brain of the dolphin is located behind the blowhole. The brains of both the chimpanzee and the goose are shown in comparison.

was not only possible but imminent, Lilly set up the Communication Research Institute (CRI) on St Thomas in the Virgin Islands,
a centre devoted to fostering human–dolphin communication
that jettisoned traditional scientific methodology for a quali-
tative experience in which he and his colleagues essentially
lived with the dolphins. In a sense, Lilly anticipated the kind of
behavioural studies pioneered by Jane Goodall and now widely
practised. But the dolphins at the CRI, an elaborately constructed

house replete with pools and waterways for the dolphins, were still essentially in a captive environment and Lilly, committed to the notion of superior dolphin intelligence, eventually released the animals and closed the Institute.

Much of Lilly's early work on dolphins, ranging from examining sleep behaviour to understanding their broad range of vocalizations, remains important and is still cited frequently in the scientific literature. But as Lilly's work continued, he moved into more speculative regions of language – which relied, questionably, on the teaching of animals to mimic human sounds – as well as on assumptions concerning intelligence. As he continued to explore the inner human mind, he embraced ideas of parapsychology and telepathy between humans and dolphins. Still, Lilly's insights were always empathetic to cetaceans, as the lyrics to the performance artist Laurie Anderson's recording, simply titled 'John Lilly', suggest:

John Lilly, the guy who says he can talk to dolphins, said he was in an aquarium and he was talking to a big whale who was swimming around and around in his tank. And the whale kept asking him questions telepathically. And one of the questions the whale kept asking was: do all oceans have walls?[8]

Although he published *Man and Dolphin* (1961) and subsequently *The Mind of the Dolphin* (1967), we remember his work, perhaps unfairly but not wholly inaccurately, from the film *The Day of the Dolphin* (1973), in which George C. Scott (himself a renegade in Hollywood) depicted Lilly attempting interspecies communication by having dolphins mimic human speech. The most memorable speech in the film is the phrase: 'Fa loves Pa', articulated by a captive dolphin that has been trained to parrot sounds produced by humans. Later in his career Lilly tried to 'enhance' his understanding of other states of consciousness through drugs such as LSD as well as in the experiences generated by isolation chambers. This part of Lilly's life was depicted in another film, *Altered States* (1980), which starred William Hurt as a Lilly-like character using the isolation experience of aquatic tanks and exotic drugs in an effort to tap into a realm of consciousness inaccessible to regular people.

Following Lilly's sensational pronouncements about dolphins, dolphin researchers kept a lower profile, seeming to retire into more academic venues. No one could match Lilly's extravagant claims and few serious cetologists were interested in having to refute grand visions to make more modest, albeit important, claims about dolphin biology and behaviour. It is worth noting, for example, the absence of any reference to Lilly in David and Melba Caldwell's highly popular *The World of the Bottlenose Dolphin* (1972). The Caldwells, who are credited with identifying the 'signature whistle' in dolphins and for creating *Cetology*, the first academic publication devoted exclusively to cetaceans, knew Lilly and his work quite well but were clearly uncomfortable with drawing attention to his work. And while many people still credit Lilly's accomplishments, including his advocacy of the Marine Mammal Protect Act of 1972, a feeling of resentment about his claims persists. Richard Ellis, a prolific author and illustrator of works about marine mammals, observes in *Dolphins and Porpoises* (1989) that Lilly's research 'has probably given more people the wrong ideas about dolphins and their intellectual abilities . . . than any other body of work in the cetological – or pseudocetological – literature'.[9]

Of course, the early days of dolphin research coincided with an increasing awareness of environmental issues, whether it was the inaugural Earth Day in 1970 or the popularity of the series

The Undersea World of Jacques Cousteau, which ran on American television in 1968–75. Cousteau played a critical role in environmental awareness, beginning with his first book *The Silent World* (1953) as well as in many subsequent books and films, including *Dolphin* (1975). And while the figure of Cousteau has been subjected to endless satire, as in the film *The Life Aquatic with Steve Zissou* (2004), in which Zissou, played by Bill Murray, detests dolphins, it is difficult to think of any other single figure who was as influential in making the public aware of marine environments.

It was also during this time that Roger Payne, who had been working on echolocation in bats and animal vocalizations, found himself studying the elaborate 'songs' generated by humpback whales. In 1970 Payne compiled several whale recordings and produced an album called *Songs of the Humpback Whale* that sold over 100,000 copies.[10] Not only was it a surprising hit but the album became a landmark event in terms of exciting public interest in wildlife studies.

Kenneth Norris, whose breakthrough work on echolocation has already been discussed, was a central figure, as a researcher, mentor and editor, in cetacean studies until his death in 1998. While Norris was working with dolphins in the early days of Marineland of the Pacific, a veterinarian named Sam Ridgway was working with the United States Navy to explore the diving physiology of dolphins, relying on one dolphin in particular, Tuffy, to determine oxygen capacity and maximum diving depth. At the University of Hawaii, Lou Herman was thoughtfully reviving the study of dolphin perception as well as 'language'. In a fascinating study, Herman was able to determine that dolphins could identify shapes using echolocation after only being exposed to them visually (using an anechoic chamber). This confirmed the transfer of information across the senses – that is, between echolocation and vision.

While the conclusion of Herman's study on the transfer of information may seem intuitive, it serves as a reminder that dolphin behaviour is so complex and so compelling that seemingly obvious patterns of behaviour deserve rigorous study. It also reflects a necessary 'correction' in some of the quick assumptions that lay audiences in particular want to make about the dolphin's intellectual abilities. The study of dolphins is, first and foremost, a zoological enterprise; in other words, dolphins are not humans in wetsuits but complexly different animals whose ostensible 'intelligence' is a factor of their environment and evolution. There has been a long-standing fascination with brain size in dolphins (and other cetaceans) that has, reductively, equated size with some generalized notion of intelligence (bigger equals smarter). But contemporary researchers such as Louis Herman, as well as the brain biologist Lori Marino, and Hal Whitehead (who studies the sperm whale), tend to discuss brain size in terms of environmental and behavioural needs. Travelling in large social groups in a three-dimensional environment while relying on a sophisticated sonar system for navigation and a refined whistle/click system for communication only begins to suggest the need for intricate neural complexity. In the fascinating article 'Cetaceans Have Complex Brains for Complex Cognition', Lori Marino and her co-authors summarize the many facets of dolphin cognition, drawing on millions of years of adaptation, and in response to environmental factors that we can't fully comprehend.[11]

> The refined capabilities of echolocation, in cetaceans at least, have important implications for social communication. These include an understanding of symbolic representations of things and events (declarative knowledge); an understanding of how things work or how to manipulate them (procedural knowledge); an understanding of the activities,

identities, and behaviours of others (social knowledge); and an understanding of one's own image, behaviour, and body parts (self knowledge). All these capabilities rest on a strong foundation of memory; investigations have demonstrated that bottlenose dolphin auditory, visual, and spatial memory are accurate and robust.[12]

Given the fact that dolphins seem to have the capacity to store and recall large quantities of knowledge, the possibility of cultural communication is compelling. The term 'cultural communication' is used to describe the transmission of acquired knowledge through generations. We conventionally think of chimpanzees teaching their offspring to use a twig to fish out termites for consumption as an example both of tool use and of cultural transmission in animals. And while a variety of animals in the wild seem to demonstrate cultural transfer of knowledge, it remains difficult to prove and controversial.[13] Vincent Janik's work on whistle matching, referred to earlier, provided evidence for the possibility of the transfer of ideas – whistles learned from another dolphin and then repeated by others – in free-ranging bottlenose dolphins. In a critical contribution to our understanding of cetacean cognition, entitled 'Culture in Whales and Dolphins', Luke Rendell and Hal Whitehead offer a broadly conceptualized rationale to argue for the persistence and transfer of knowledge across generations in a variety of cetacean species.[14] They note, for example, that female killer whales in the Subantarctic teach their offspring how to temporarily strand themselves in order to hunt for seals.[15] Although specific instances of 'intelligence' we see in dolphins may not necessarily have exact analogues in the human experience, the mechanisms, the capacity, the exchange and the plasticity of cetacean intelligence are, to say the least, familiar.

Dolphins are clearly intelligent, but one of the common measures for intellectual complexity among animals, ranging from
crows to chimpanzees, is tool use. Until recently, no dolphin
species had been observed using a tool, but observers in Shark
Bay, Australia, noticed that dolphins were foraging along the
ocean bottom while 'wearing' basket sponges on their beaks. As
it turns out, the sharp rocks, sand and broken coral that com-
pose the sea floor provides a very convenient resting area for the
bottom-dwelling barred sandperch, a species that lacks a swim
bladder and is thus both more difficult to spot by echolocation
and more nutritious because of its denser body. In smoother
environments (such as the sandy sea floor of the Bahamas) it is
easy to forage for bottom-dwellers, but the dolphins in Shark Bay
would quickly damage their beaks if they foraged in the sharp
sediment without protection. And so the basket sponge is used
to stir up the sediment, revealing the perch, which are snapped
up once the tool is dropped. The behaviour is more common
among females and appears to be taught to the younger dolphins
by experienced adults.

We also understand, intuitively, that dolphins are self-aware,
yet a statement like this requires more than intuition or anecdotal
observation. Recent mirror studies, by which a mark is placed on
a dolphin that is then given access to a mirror, have confirmed
that dolphins are very much aware of the position of foreign or
unfamiliar marks on their bodies, and recognize their image in a
mirror as a reflection of themselves as individuals.[16]

While we might not be surprised that dolphins can, in fact,
identify themselves in a mirror, establishing that fact empirically
is yet another crucial step in teasing out the group's cognitive
abilities. The mirror test – which elephants also passed recently

– is hardly the most robust measure of animal 'intelligence' and behavioural complexity, but it has become a benchmark in animal studies. Perhaps that test and others should remind us how primitive human measures are for quantifying and even describing the degree of sophistication that we observe in animals such as dolphins. We share nothing, or at least very little, of the experiential world of other animals, especially dolphins, and so every test we design is necessarily constructed on anthropocentric criteria.

The limitations of our understanding are underscored by recent observations, in Hawaiian waters, of an interaction between a humpback whale and a bottlenose dolphin. The whale was observed to gently raise the dolphin completely out of the water, after which the dolphin slid down the whale's rostrum back into the ocean. No aggressive behaviour was observed and so the assumption is that this represented willing social play between species which, while certainly not unique in animals, has not been recorded in two such divergent groups of cetaceans.[17] It's hard to know what to make of this interaction, but it does suggest that we can anticipate many changes in the way that we think about the nuances and complexities of intelligence, play, and interspecies behaviour.

Still, even as we look ahead to future insights, there are many ways in which we describe, engage with and explore animal behaviour. In Donna Haraway's book about companion species, such as dogs, *When Species Meet*, she articulates the very personal criteria that help define animal–human relationships, while the philosopher Jacques Derrida, in *The Animal that Therefore I Am*, recognizes the impossibility of engaging with animals without sorting through the complex social, religious and political constructions that historically have been used to separate ourselves from the animal world.[18]

Although philosophical approaches are helpful as we navigate our understanding of other species, such as dogs and cats, dolphins introduce particularly complex – if not unprecedented – dimensions to interspecies relations. The human–dolphin connection is multifaceted and while the stories that tie humans and dolphins together may seem fanciful, many are grounded in actual practice. Historically, for example, there are many records of dolphins 'fishing' cooperatively with humans. In the fishing town of Laguna on the southern coast of Brazil, commercial fishermen have been observed working cooperatively with dolphins, a practice that dates back to 1847, according to local records. In general, only a small number of dolphins out of a large pod of 100–200 may participate in the herding of mullet and other fish into a line of fisherman holding small nets. These are, according to the fishermen, the 'good' dolphins, who manoeuvre and signal the fishermen in what is probably a mutually learned set of behaviours, such as the most convenient moment to draw in the nets. There are, however, 'bad' dolphins, generally individuals, that act as spoilers, disrupting the schools

An encounter between a bottlenose dolphin and a humpback that appears to be interspecies' play.

of fish. It is not entirely clear what benefit the cooperating dolphins derive from their herding behaviour, but it is possible that as they knock the fish against the net, more of the prey are confused and those that are not drawn in by the fishermen are more easily captured by the dolphins themselves. The practice is ongoing and has been recorded in the popular documentary *Wild Secrets: Aquatic Animals* (2010).

Fishermen in Myanmar rely on the Irrawaddy dolphins to help gather fish. In this case, the fishermen remain in canoes and tap on the hull to 'call' the dolphins. The fishermen then slap the water with paddles and, using a combination of guttural vocalizations and the sound of the nets dangling alongside the boat, prompt the dolphins to swim in tightening circles around the boat, thus herding the fish into the range of the nets. On the Atlantic coast of Mauritania, the Imraguen people also fish cooperatively with dolphins. The fishermen slap the water vigorously to scare the fish into leaping out of the water, but this also attracts local dolphins, who help corral the already panicked fish into waiting nets.[19] In more recent years, however, as industrialized fishing has been introduced into the region, the dolphins now face a potential food shortage.

The humpback dolphin.

In South America, explorers have long described cooperative catches made with bottlenose dolphins, and local 'artisanal' fishermen are known to have fished cooperatively with Amazon river dolphins. In Mauritania local groups fish with the Atlantic humpback dolphins (*Sousa teuszii*). Fishermen on the Irrawady communicate with the dolphins using both audio and visual signals during fishing.[20] The numbers of fish caught per outing often tripled when dolphins were involved in the process.[21] Longstanding accounts from Moreton Bay, Australia, an area where bottlenose dolphins can be found in great numbers, describe cooperative fishing between the dolphins and the aboriginal peoples. Cooperative interactions, especially in fishing, generally involve a sub-group of a pod, if not the entire pod itself. Other forms of interaction, usually involve a lone dolphin or perhaps a pair.

Cooperative fishing, a 'mutualistic' behaviour in which both parties benefit, had to evolve over many years. Not only do animals and humans have to gain each other's trust, but each partner must train the other in the techniques and cues that bring about a mutually beneficial outcome. In both modern and ancient examples of cooperation, we inevitably become aware of the act of cooperation well after the actual evolution of the process has taken place. But the evidence of cooperative interactions is nevertheless there and the records of mutual assistance go far back in history. Among the earliest recorded instances of cooperative fishing between humans and dolphins is Pliny's account, in which dolphins off the southern coast of France herded fish (probably mullet) into the nets of waiting fishermen. Pliny provides little detail so we cannot know whether the dolphins were working in concert with the fishermen or whether their catch increased because the dolphins were simply herding schools of fish into a constricted area. Again, the process is almost certainly a mutually

learned behaviour that has evolved (culturally) over a very long period of time.[22]

It is probably more common, when considering dolphin–human interactions, to hear of animals that tend to linger around a beach or a cove and befriend the local inhabitants. Many wild dolphins, generally loners, have been known to swim into shallow waters and mingle with human bathers. A number of these stories come from New Zealand, where perhaps the most famous 'friendly' dolphin was Opo who, in 1955 and 1996, played freely with children and adults at the beach in the town of Oponini. Opo became famous and was the inspiration for songs, stories and a statue, but in 1956 she was found dead in a crevice, possibly the victim of explosives used by local fishermen. More recently, another New Zealand bottlenose dolphin, Moko, appeared at Mahia Beach on the North Island of New Zealand. Attributed with helping a pair of pygmy sperm whales trapped near a sandbar, Moko was observed – by two individuals who themselves were trying to rescue the whales – to have led them through a shallow channel to open water. But Moko was also responsible for preventing a swimmer with whom he had been playing, from returning to shore, until rowers could get to the stranded woman and rescue her.

Another bottlenose dolphin, named 'Fungi', although a bit more reserved than Moko, has been a constant feature of Ireland's Dingle Harbour (Co. Kerry) since 1984. Fungi, who must be in his late thirties, cavorts with local fishermen and tourist boats and has been honoured with a bronze sculpture – no less popular than Fungi himself – on the quayside.

There is a temptation to interpret the 'friendly' behaviour of dolphins (and killer whales) as a gesture of unequivocal good will and even as a rational understanding of humans. The reality is, of course, that all dolphins – no matter how friendly – are in fact large and powerful animals that despite their playfulness, are undomesticated. What's more, dolphins that frequent tourist areas, whether bays or shallows, are themselves subject to harm from boats, nets, fishing hooks and human malice.

Such malice was directed at another renowned dolphin, Pelorus Jack, a Risso's dolphin that became known (and beloved) between 1888 and 1912 for accompanying boats navigating Cook's Strait, the isthmus between the North and South Islands of New Zealand. Although called Jack, the gender of the dolphin – who at 4 metres was quite long and almost certainly weighed over 540 kilograms (13 ft; 1,200 lb) – was never certain. It is clear though that this dolphin escaped a rifle shot in 1904, which led to special legislation in New Zealand, an Order-in-Council, protecting him, until he finally disappeared in 1912. What motivated Pelorus Jack to serve as a guide is not clear, and he seems to have restricted his activities to open water, never consorting with swimmers. But an eerie legend about Pelorus Jack does persist: it is said that he never again helped guide the ss *Penguin*, the ship from which the notorious shot was fired.[23] And, for those who choose to believe the darker side of the story, the fact that the

Penguin was ultimately wrecked in 1909 in Cook's Strait, with a loss of 72 lives, lends an ominous perspective to Pelorus Jack's legacy. Still, Pelorus Jack has remained a positive folkloric figure in New Zealand and has consistently been the subject of folk songs extolling his prowess as a guide and his dedication to stewarding ships through Cook's Strait.[24]

Among the dolphins that consort with fisherman, none are better known than the dolphins of Monkey Mia, a tourist resort considerably north of Perth, Australia. In the 1960s local fishermen began the practice of throwing a bit of their catch to the local bottlenose dolphins, drawing them into the clear shallow waters. The routine took hold and the dolphins became regular visitors, attracting curious neighbours and eventually tourists. The feeding still continues under the supervision of the Department of Environment and Conservation, and Monkey Mia is not only a highly visited tourist attraction but home to the Shark Bay Research Foundation, an important centre for research on bottlenose dolphins.[25] As in so many other cases of ecotourism, the paradox is that the infrastructure that is required to house, feed, as well as provide drinking water and plumbing for tourists, often despoils the very environment the tourists have come to observe.

The many paradoxes of dolphin tourism, whether at Monkey Mia or even commercial oceanaria, are difficult to solve but not hard to understand. Humans find dolphins so deeply intriguing that we will find as many ways as possible, often to the detriment of the animals, to be close to them. What compels us is not absolutely clear, but it owes something to a sense of receptivity that we feel when watching dolphins. This is particularly true of the bottlenose dolphin, the species we know and actually understand best of all. That all dolphins strike us as intelligent is only to say that the more we interact with them, the more we find that is new and interesting. It is easy to see, in the sophisticated and complex relationships among dolphins, behaviours that seem analogous to our own. That too, however, is a paradox, because dolphins are so different from humans that drawing analogies cannot be 'right'. But proper or not, scientists and laypersons alike find these animals irresistible and are compelled to pursue questions about the dolphin's intelligence, behaviours and abilities.

5 Dolphin Dangers: Tuna, Predation, Pollution, Exploitation

My thoughts turned frequently to the dolphins. Where were
they now? What were they doing in that incomprehensible
darkness of the sea and greater darkness of the night?
Diane Ackerman, *Deep Play* (2000)

Despite the many examples of cooperative fishing between
humans and dolphins, fishing has always presented some
danger to dolphins. Dolphins have, of course, been 'fished' as a
source of food in areas, such as Japan, where dolphin meat is
prized by some. The flesh of the pink dolphin or Amazon river
dolphin, while not consumed as meat, is prized as bait for a local
species of catfish, which fetches a good price in cities such as
Bogotá. The killing serves two purposes, because the local fisherman also consider the dolphins a competitor for fish.[1] Scientists,
such as António Miguel Miguéis, are trying to educate fishermen
about the Amazon river dolphin, suggesting among other things
that they use pig meat as bait, in an effort to prevent the slaughter
that is taking place.

Surely one of the most serious concerns about the killing of
dolphins, setting aside hunting them for food, has focused on
the tuna industry, particularly in the Tropical Eastern Pacific
ocean. It is there that dolphins (spotted, spinner and common)
are accompanied by schools of yellowfin tuna; thus dolphins
are one of the means by which fishermen know where to find
the tuna, and in consequence were being caught or taken up in
the very purse-seine nets being used to catch the tuna. Euphem-
istically called a 'bycatch', the estimates of how many dolphins
have been killed in this manner vary, but the number – since

about 1950 – may run as high as 7 to 8 million. The tuna industry had essentially ignored this problem for decades, arguing that if any animals were killed, the numbers were insignificant. But in 1988 a young graduate student in biological studies by the name of Samuel LaBudde shipped aboard a Panamanian-flagged tuna fishing vessel under contract to one of the major canneries. LaBudde videotaped the purse-seine process, revealing dozens of dolphins caught in the nets, some already drowned, some caught by their beaks and flippers only to have them broken as they were hauled well above the ship.[2] When released, the video offered conclusive proof that our enormous appetite for tuna was being satisfied at the expense of tens of thousands of dolphin lives. In 1990, H. J. Heinz, the parent company of StarKist Tuna, announced that it would not sell 'any tuna caught in association with dolphins'; their announcement was quickly followed by similar declarations by the brands Bumble Bee and Chicken of the Sea. The 'dolphin safe' label, which manufacturers originally placed on their products individually, was adopted by the United States Department of Commerce in 1990. Since then the average mortality rate for dolphins has dropped to fewer than 2,000 deaths per year, though other oceanic wildlife such as albatross and sharks may still be caught in the nets.

Dolphins are also subject to less direct, but no less lethal, threats from humans in various forms of pollution. Squid are one of the primary foods in the dolphin diet and plastic debris, including bags, can resemble squid; if consumed in sufficient numbers, the plastic items will cause death. Such pollutants are a problem for all aquatic animals and should indicate the need for greater control and vigilance of waste disposal and simple littering in seaside environments. But even more disturbing are the high levels of 'persistent organic pollutants (POPS) including legacy POPS (PCBS, chlordanes, mirex, DDTS, HCB, and dieldrin),

The official, though not the only, insignia for dolphin-safe tuna.

and polybrominated diphenyl ether (PBDE) flame retardants that are commonly washed into aquatic environments'. These chemicals were found in '300 blubber biopsy samples from coastal and near shore/estuarine male bottlenose dolphins (*Tursiops truncatus*)' on the Eastern Seaboard.[3] 'Samples were from 14 locations including urban and rural estuaries and near a Superfund site in Brunswick, Georgia, contaminated with the PCB formulation Aroclor 1268.' These carcinogens, which also have significant developmental effects, have been accumulating in dolphins and may be leading to higher mortality rates both of adults and newborns. These pollutants pose problems principally for dolphins themselves, but in Japan, where dolphins are still consumed by humans, the aggregation of these pollutants offers another serious rationale to ban the hunting of dolphins and the consumption of their flesh. As top predators it is not surprising that the concentration of chemical pollutants that are pervasive in the environment should be extremely high, but these concentration levels are not merely a threat to dolphins but to every organism. However localized or restricted we believe these sources of pollution to be (such as in capped landfills, or Superfund 'sites'), the concentrations we find in highly peripatetic animals like dolphins should be a careful reminder of how quickly pollutants spread and how rapidly they achieve threatening levels in the body.

Perhaps the most sobering note with respect to the exploitation of dolphins has been the capture and killing of dolphins in the town of Taiji in Japan, depicted in the award-winning documentary *The Cove* (2009). Filmed by Ric O'Barry, the former *Flipper* trainer, and Louis Psihoyos, the movie records an annual practice in the village of Taiji whereby dolphins are herded into a secluded cove and are either netted, or speared and killed, in order to serve two primary markets: 1) worldwide oceanaria looking for dolphins to perform in shows; and 2) the profitable market for dolphin meat (even though the toxins in the meat, as O'Barry observes, should preclude its consumption). If it is shocking to most readers that dolphins are being butchered for meat, it may be worth recalling that as recently as 1964 the *Encyclopaedia Britannica* noted that 'dolphins are edible'. Even the most conservative estimates, from the Japanese government, indicate that about 1,500 dolphins are killed annually by the drive in Taiji. Filmed surreptitiously, against the will of the Taiji fishermen, the documentary has been controversial but has also played a significant role in the move to save dolphins. Despite the somewhat overwrought poster for the film, evoking a Christ-like image of a diver suffering the little children (here, dolphins) to come unto him, the movie is powerful enough to resist sentimentalism. The issues covered are very serious for anyone interested in animal welfare and O'Barry, while not yet successful at stopping the hunt, has garnered considerable support worldwide and even in Japan to move towards a moratorium on the killing.

No doubt there are also other dolphin killings worldwide, but the scope of the drive at Taiji is astonishing. That dolphins, which are held in great esteem elsewhere as cooperative fishing partners or simply as animals that warrant respect and admiration, should be slaughtered so cruelly in the modern era is shocking. There is a long history of abuse of dolphins, and their special qualities, including an affinity for people, have paradoxically made them even more vulnerable to human activity.

In a similar vein, the Canadian Broadcasting Corporation (CBC) examined the worldwide trade in dolphins in its hour-long *Dolphin Dealer* (2008). The documentary follows the exploits of Christopher Porter, a former dolphin trainer who captures dolphins for use in aquaria, petting pools and dolphin encounters (where people can swim with dolphins), earning more than $100,000 per dolphin. Ric O'Barry has been trying to shut down Porter's trafficking network, and is central to the documentary.

To turn from the horrors of Taiji to the use of dolphins in the military is admittedly an unfair transition, but it is critical to take a look at the adoption of dolphins for military service. The tractability and intelligence of dolphins, combined with a growing awareness of the ability of these animals to use echolocation to 'see' shape and density, has been apparent to military strategists in both the U.S. and Russia for decades. The U.S. Navy, in fact, has been using dolphins for research and for deployment since the early 1960s when, according to official histories, the hydrodynamics of a Pacific white-sided dolphin were studied in order to learn more about underwater resistance and drag. Scientists like Sam Ridgway, who worked for the Navy Marine Mammal Program in San Diego, produced a good deal of research that remains central to our understanding of dolphins.[4] Other marine mammals, including sea lions, were recruited by the Navy for the retrieval and identification of underwater objects, but the programme was predominantly devoted to dolphins. Still today, dolphins are used to identify and mark underwater mines with floating buoy devices so that they can be found and neutralized by appropriate personnel. Another project, 'force protection' training, prepares dolphins to stand sentinel against intruders by attaching buoys to their air tanks; these markers would then rise to the surface, alerting navy personnel to the location of the interlopers. Most recently dolphins were used in the Iraq War to search for sea mines, which respond to large metal objects (such as ships) and not to smaller animals such as sharks or dolphins swimming by. Thus, according to the Navy, the mines present almost no threat to the dolphins. Well equipped for transporting dolphins around the world, the Navy must also attach

A u.s. Navy dolphin equipped with a locating 'pinger' on its flipper.

'pingers' to the animals, who find themselves performing tasks in unfamiliar waters where they might easily get lost.

The Russian equivalent of the Navy Marine Mammal Program, based at the Kazachya Bay Naval Base on the Black Sea, was shut down in the 1990s, although several of the animals remained to perform for tourists or to provide dolphin therapy.[5] The dolphins were then sold by their former trainer to Iran.[6] The u.s. Navy has denied that any of its animals have been trained to inflict harm on other individuals or, in the case of so-called kamikaze missions, on themselves. Wide-eyed sceptics have expressed fear that dolphins have been trained to jam sonar transmissions, shoot poison darts and actually plant mines, but these concerns are fraught with many difficulties and probably owe as much to video game scenarios as they do to reality.

Needless to say, the u.s. Navy's use of marine mammals in general and dolphins in particular has met with some resistance by a variety of protest groups. The Navy has countered that opposition by arguing that their animals are very well taken care of, and that having invested intense amounts of labour and training in each animal in their 'ranks', there is every incentive to keep them out of the way of life-threatening harm. Nevertheless, ethical issues about the use of dolphins, belugas, killer whales and seals for military purposes will not go away very easily.

6 Dolphins and Popular Culture

Like any other fictional character, Flipper existed only in art.
Though he seemed as real as life – or more real, actually as
art is supposed to be – Flipper was an illusion, an elaborate
fabrication.
Ric O'Barry, *Behind the Dolphin Smile* (1988)

It is almost impossible to discuss any subject involving dolphins
without some reference to the television icon, Flipper. The dolphin
character first appeared in a film, *Flipper* (1963), starring Chuck
Connors, and eventually led to a television series which ran from
1947 to 1964. Although the 'Flipper Generation' may be dying out
with the baby-boomers, the Flipper 'brand' somehow seems to
persist. *Flipper* was a natural successor to a trend in television
shows like *Lassie* (1954–73), *The Adventures of Rin Tin Tin* (1954–9)
and *Skippy the Bush Kangaroo* (1966–8), in which an adventure-
prone boy befriends an intelligent and heroic animal. Through
the advent of underwater cinematography and the creation of
facilities like Marine Studios, it was possible to add dolphins
to the list of boy-with-animal programmes. The idea intrigued
the producer Ivan Tors, who had a penchant for animal dramas
such as *Daktari* and *Cowboy in Africa* as well as the underwater
adventures *Sea Hunt* (1958–61) and the less well-known *Aqua-
nauts* (1960–61).

Flipper, which was filmed at the Miami Seaquarium by Tors,
followed a widowed marine park ranger in Florida, Porter Ricks,
and his two sons Sandy and Bud, who have befriended a solitary
male dolphin (played by an array of female dolphins) by the
name of Flipper. The show exuded an intensely masculinized
environment, where the brainy and, yes, phallic, Flipper was a

heroic extension of three male egos, all in different stages of development. Flipper's inevitable triumph in each episode extended, in one way or another, the virility (and sometimes sensitivity) of the central male cast members. Despite the centrality of the Flipper character, very little attention was paid to Flipper as a member of a larger group of animals called dolphins; in fact the show, pairing the lone Flipper with human companions, imparted the mistaken notion that the bottlenose dolphin is a solitary species. Thus Flipper was rarely shown with other dolphins or depicted hunting for fish, and was apparently confined to a life of bachelorhood, having earned the affection of three human pals. Although the television series was cancelled after its third year in 1967, the impact of *Flipper* on viewers and American culture at large was so indelible and long-lasting that Flipper is probably still the most iconic representation of all dolphins. A commemorative statue to Mitzi, one of the dolphins who played Flipper, can still be found in Grassy Key, at what was once the Flipper Sea School and is now the Dolphin Research Center. *Mad* magazine parodied *Flipper* (as 'Flapper', October 1965) in the very early stages of the show's broad success.

After a hiatus from television – though always invoked in dolphin presentations in aquaria – the Flipper 'franchise' was officially revived in an hour-long *Flipper* television series that was produced in 1995. Ostensibly set in Florida, the show, which also only lasted three years, was filmed in Australia and boasted a more scientifically driven plot that attempted to incorporate more findings about dolphin behaviour. Sandwiched between the two *Flippers* was a programme in 1989, written by Peter Benchley, called *Dolphin Cove*. Although an American production, it was actually set in Australia, where a widowed scientist and his children settle to allow for his research on dolphins. By the 1980s, when this show was produced, a New Age sensibility about dolphins

The cast from TV's *Flipper* featured in a Gold Key comic book.

had established itself as legitimate. Thus the scientist's daughter, who has been unable to speak since the death of her mother, discovers that she has the ability to communicate with and even speak to dolphins. The notion that the dolphin has the 'power to heal', a common theme in New Age representations of the animal, remains deeply lodged in the popular view of dolphins and, as we shall see, has inspired what is typically called the 'dolphin experience', or more frequently, 'dolphin therapy'.

The brief appearance in 1965 of the Japanese animated television show *Marine Boy* captured enough of an international audience to warrant a quick look here. The show centred on the inevitable pairing of a young boy and his dolphin pal, Splasher, who in tandem – as the theme song explains – would inevitably 'foil the foe'. Modelled, no doubt, after *Astro Boy*, another Japanese anime production that was far more successful, *Marine Boy* barely made it through two seasons and yet it nevertheless reflected a new appreciation, albeit in a commercial context, for dolphins and the environment.

A striking but relatively short-lived television show of the '90s was *seaQuest DSV*, which followed the adventures of an enormous submarine or Deep-Submergence Vehicle. Among the crew, a jumble of scientists and navy personnel, is yet another solitary dolphin, named Darwin. The programme reflected continued interest in the work of John Lilly; Darwin, for example, inhabits an extensive network of aquatic corridors on board the ship not unlike the structure of Lilly's lab-home on St Thomas. What's more, the crew members are able to employ a translation device that allowed Darwin's whistles and clicks to be heard as English, a variant of Lilly's attempt to have dolphins 'speak' English themselves. We can only assume that human voices, when translated back to Darwin by the same machine, are heard as whistles and clicks, but this side of the conversation was never replicated for

Norman Mingo's interpretation of a dolphin performance from *Mad* magazine (October 1965).

No. 98
Oct. '65

OUR PRICE
30¢
STILL
CHEAP

viewers. Still, it was through this computer-generated dialogue that Darwin receives instructions allowing him (predictably) to save the ship, the crew and often, humanity.

It seems likely that dolphins will always have some role in science fiction, given the interest in their intelligence, their social nature and of course the many New Age myths associated with their brain size, their ability to communicate and their 'spiritual essence'. Science fiction often runs with these characteristics in order to reveal a dystopian world in which dolphins are poorly treated. Perhaps the most exploited dolphin in literature and film is Jones, the dolphin at the heart of William Gibson's story 'Johnny Mnemonic' (1981), adapted into a film of the same name in 1995. Jones, who has been modified into a cyborg by the Navy, now floats alone in an enclosure where he is guarded by a futuristic underground movement. Gibson's Jones also incorporates the sensibility of the 1980s, bringing together in one creature the idea of a hyper-intellectual dolphin that ultimately saves humanity despite having been oppressed and exploited by human tyranny.

In the award-winning novel *Startide Rising* (1983), David Brin offers his own version of hyper-intellectual dolphins in the distant future (2489 CE). These animals, however, must be enhanced or 'uplifted' in order to be capable of operating a spaceship, but the dolphins are still not fully up to human standards and can, the novel reveals, revert to a more primitive or 'instinctual' state. Whatever the outcome, there remains in Brin and other writers an idealistic sense of optimism for some untapped potential in dolphins that, when realized, oddly enough makes them more like humans than some augmented version of themselves *as* dolphins.

One of the reasons that optimism is associated with dolphins is their ostensible smile, a feature absent in their larger cousin, the killer whale. As I indicated earlier, it is rare indeed that dolphins are presented in a negative light, but orcas – which are also known to kill mammalian prey – have not always been so fortunate. Often considered large and rapacious, medieval illustrations made them seem ugly and malevolent. Although that is no longer the case, popular sentiment about killer whales has changed only recently, and even now it is tinged with fear. A fascinating example of the hatred of the killer whale is apparent in an early episode (*c.* 1963) of the popular American television show *Sea Hunt*. The show, essentially an underwater detective programme, was ahead of its time in that each show concluded by having the star, Lloyd Bridges, sign off with a pithy insight concerning saving the oceans. Still, in the episode 'Killer Whale' (aired 22 March 1958), which concludes with Bridges reminding viewers that 'three-fifths of the world is covered by the sea, [yet] how little most of us know about that underwater world', Bridges's character Mike Nelson maligns the killer whale as 'the world's most savage monster' that often 'capsizes boats', and prefers 'warm-blooded prey and often human beings'. In the episode, a rogue killer whale swallows an unfortunate diver 'in one gulp' and is eventually killed with a harpoon gun, as Nelson vows 'they ought to be destroyed, every last one of them'. Exciting rhetoric perhaps, but hardly an enlightened view of that unknown underwater world *Sea Hunt* ostensibly promoted. Another interesting facet of this rather confused episode is that the above-water shots of the killer are of an orca, while in underwater scenes a pilot whale, and sometimes a shark, serve as stand-ins. Whether audiences actually accepted this rather absurd back-and-forth between two different genera, never mind species, is fascinating to consider. In what ways have we become better consumers of animal images and animal life histories?

By way of apology for maligning killer whales in *Sea Hunt*, Ivan Tors (who produced the show) developed and produced the

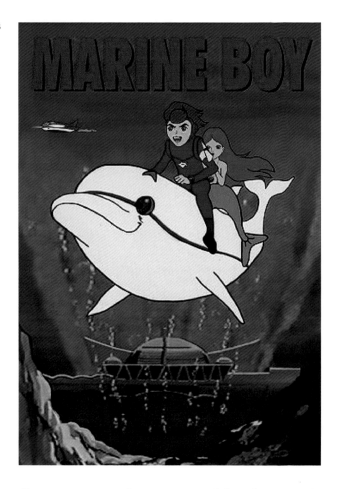

film *Namu* in 1966.[1] The movie emerged from the rescue of a
killer whale that was caught in a fishing net near the small town
of Namu, north of Vancouver Island. The rescued whale, named
after the village, is depicted in the film as the grieving mate of
a female heartlessly killed by local fishermen, none of whom –

incidentally – appear to be Inuit. Namu finds himself in a cove owned by a marine biologist, who gradually converts the anti-whale hostility of the local community into appreciation, acceptance and admiration of killer whales in general. Tors completes his apology by depicting a widowed woman who lost her husband to an orca swim with and effectively befriend Namu. *Namu* was accompanied by an eco-friendly theme song, titled 'The Ballad of Namu the Killer Whale', by Tom Glazer. The song enjoyed moderate success, invoking an environmental sensibility associated with 1960s counter-culture:

Live and let live, let Nature be your teacher,
Respect the life of your fellow creature,
Live and let live, whatever you do,
And always remember the killer whale, Namu.

Alas, while the fictional Namu was released back into the wild, Namu himself died within the year. Shamu, the female captured to accompany him, never got along with Namu and was sold to SeaWorld of San Diego, where she performed for ten years without incident. She was put into 'retirement' in 1971 after biting Anne Eckis, an employee – but not a trainer – who had been hired to ride on her back while wearing a bikini.[2] The objective was a glamorous publicity shot, but the event backfired when Eckis fell off Shamu, was pushed around, the whale then grasped her leg and 'returned' her to the other trainer. The puncture wounds were not severe, but the incident led to a lawsuit and increased vigilance for trainers and others interacting with killer whales. It was noted by many that Shamu's behaviour, which might have easily been more violent, could be explained by the fact that the orca was not accustomed to familiar humans in wetsuits much less strangers in colourful bikinis.

While the movie *Namu* attempted to represent a killer whale that was docile in its grief, the horror film *Orca* (1977) envisions yet another killer whale – also grieving for its mate – as a vicious and single-minded predator. The whale's violence is prompted by the actions of Captain Nolan (Richard Harris), a reckless fisherman who kills a pregnant female orca only to be pursued relentlessly by its male partner. And while there is some effort to elicit empathy for the whale (the victim of Nolan's villainy), the animal is eventually depicted as insanely vengeful, brutal and powerful beyond natural expectations.

If the cinematic career of cetaceans (revived briefly in 1986 with the appearance of humpback whales in *Star Trek IV*) has moved in any direction, it has been towards documentaries. Jacques Cousteau featured a variety of dolphins in his *Undersea World* series, and more recently National Geographic's *Dolphins: The Wild Side* (1999) took the unusual tack of revealing that the species has a wild or 'dark' side. Once perceived as 'gods', the 'soaring spirits of the sea', the other side of dolphins emerges in the film: 'Cunning, powerful and relentless, dolphins are consummate predators.' In 2000, IMAX cinemas screened a very upbeat and dynamic feature, simply titled *Dolphins*, by MacGillivray Freeman Films, that travelled the world to explain and present some of the more recent research on dolphins by individuals such as Kathleen Dudzinski, Bernd Würsig, Louis Herman and Alejandro Acevedo-Gutiérrez.

Perhaps because of a growing angst about keeping dolphins in captivity, Hollywood adopted a different tone when dealing with cetaceans. A bellwether for this new approach was the film *Free Willy* (1993), a huge hit that explored the problems of keeping orcas in captivity. Following the well-trodden convention of boy-meets-dolphin, the movie depicts the close bond formed between a young and disaffected foster child (Jesse), whose soulmate just happens to be Willy, a whale violently wrested from his family in the wild. With corporate greed as a backdrop, the plot moves both Willy and Jesse towards self-fulfilment and liberty, all against the soaring strains of Michael Jackson's 'Will You Be There'. Keiko, the whale who played Willy, was captured off the coast of Iceland in 1979 and had already endured a brief stint at an aquarium in Canada and then a move to Mexico City in 1985. One of the outcomes of the film was an actual movement to liberate Keiko from his less-than-satisfactory home in Reino Aventura, the Mexico City aquarium. At 3,600 kilos (4 tons), Keiko was certainly difficult to move, but the 'Free Keiko' movement led to his being transported (on a modified Boeing C-17 aeroplane) to the Oregon Coast Aquarium in 1996. Keiko's adventure continued as he was returned to Iceland's

A trainer riding on the chest of a killer whale.

Klettsvik Bay in 1998 with the ambition of returning him to the wild. Unfortunately, Keiko never made the transition back to the wild and responsibility for his welfare fell to the Ocean Futures Society to monitor and feed him. He beached himself and subsequently died in 2004, ostensibly from pneumonia, although his general health had declined drastically.

Free Willy and Keiko's travails notwithstanding, the general public has on the whole been eager to pay to see whales and dolphins perform in captivity for decades. It is estimated that between 1972 and 1994, over 2,000 dolphins were captured for display in zoos and aquaria. As a consequence, many more children have been exposed to live (albeit captive) dolphins, killer whales and beluga whales, and *Flipper* is slowly being replaced by the 'live' experience. In most cases these aquaria provide a show (often very heavily scripted) in which the dolphins or whales perform tricks that reveal their skills, but rarely provide any lasting information about their biology or behaviour. Oceanaria patrons walk away without a clear sense of how the animals differ in appearance, how gender is distinguished, how one can tell that dolphins are mammals, and dozens of other simple concepts which they are actually eager to learn.

To satisfy public interest in a 'hands-on' dolphin experience, some oceanaria still maintain very controversial 'petting pools', where patrons can approach the animals, housed in shallow pools, and pet or stroke them. The petting pools, which are small and ringed by very vocal children and adults, are stressful even to observers; so it is not surprising that petting dolphins have been known to be aggressive towards patrons and more than a few patrons have been bitten or raked. Furthermore, the amount of debris that can be found in petting pools is shocking, ranging from cardboard containers to sunglasses and bottles. To be sure, many patrons are not particularly concerned about the welfare of the animals, but overall, petting pools reflect a failure on the part of the oceanarium to inculcate sensitivity towards or awareness of the dolphins themselves.

The entire question of whether dolphins, beluga and killer whales should be kept in captivity, although always controversial, has recently come under scrutiny in a u.s. government-sponsored study. Many groups worldwide, including the Humane Society, the Dolphin Project and the Whale and Dolphin Conservation Society, are opposed to maintaining cetaceans in marine aquaria.[3] Yet currently there are close to 200 oceanaria worldwide that keep dolphins, primarily bottlenose and spinner, which means that there are probably close to 1,000 dolphins in captivity, to say nothing of orcas.

Of the many other delphinids that are popular as tourist attractions, the killer whale ranks first, but some oceanaria also house pilot whales and beluga whales. The whales and dolphins that are on view do not always account for the number of animals housed 'behind the scenes'. Certain stage names given to dolphins or whales, like 'Splash', can last beyond the lifetime of a single animal, so that if an animal dies in captivity, the name artfully lives on in its successor. Animals, especially killer whales, that are considered aggressive or non-sociable, are kept in holding tanks while their more tractable companions perform. But even whales that appear to be docile have proven themselves unpredictable. On 24 February 2010, Dawn Brancheau, an experienced trainer at SeaWorld of Orlando, was killed by Tilikum, the 'oldest and largest killer whale in captivity'.[4] The whale itself was apparently kept in isolation during non-show hours because of a prior record of aggressive behaviour. But the practice of isolation, as Naomi Rose of the Humane Society has noted, can itself be problematic; she argues that this kind of isolation is, for social animals, debilitating.[5] The sheer size of killer whales makes captivity even more problematic than it is for dolphins, although both groups are accustomed to vast home ranges in the wild. In a recent book, *Death at Seaworld*, exploring the life of Tilikum and the circumstances of Brancheau's death, the journalist David Kirby considers the practicality of captivity in general.[6]

Other forms of exposure to dolphins include tourist spots that offer adults and children a 'dolphin experience', where individuals can enter the water (usually a penned enclosure) and swim with the animals. Supposedly for the therapeutic benefit of autistic children, these facilities attract a wide array of tourists interested in the dolphin 'experience'. But what exactly a dolphin experience offers clients is not always clear. Much of popular literature characterizes the experience of swimming with dolphins as 'spiritual': the presence of another intelligence is said to elevate the human spirit, even though the 'experience' typically requires the source of that intelligence to remain in captivity.

There is no doubt that swimming with dolphins, whether in the wild or in captivity, can be a dramatic experience. Even the strongest and most agile swimmer cannot keep track of four to five animals circling and diving in the water with extraordinary speed and agility. And dolphins, even the smallest ones, are impressively large in the water. They are also impressively noisy. A swimmer is not only immersed in water but, more important, in a medium of sound filled with echolocation clicks, burst pulses, whistles and perhaps even jaw claps. In short, swimming with dolphins can be as distressing as it is idyllic.

The noise produced by dolphins in an aquarium is intensified by the fact that pools are made of concrete and glass, which are typically smooth and reflective. Thus the sounds that might dissipate in an ocean setting, replete with sand and organic life, will have a longer reflective life in a pool. Pools are also maintained by extensive pumping and filtration equipment, which produces sounds constantly from which the animals cannot escape. In the sea, sounds can dissipate over distances but in artificial pools the reflective surfaces keep sounds 'alive' for much longer periods of time. Because hygiene is so important, pools must be kept clean, and there is therefore generally very little sand, coral or vegetative matter to absorb or deflect sound. This can hardly be an advantageous situation for captive animals, especially given that Whitlow Au and other scientists have argued that the increasing levels of noise in actual ocean environments may in fact be harmful to marine mammals and have a significant negative impact on their health. Cautionary notices like these are difficult to assess, but surely the austere settings of pools and the constant input of mechanical sounds – to say nothing of the sounds of audiences, trainers and ambient noises – must have some effect on the animals.

As an entertainment product (if you will), dolphins – whether as performers in aquaria, as petting subjects in pools or as therapeutic agents – have demonstrated the ability to attract wide audiences and provide substantial revenue for enterprising aquariums. The lingering questions about the ethics of maintaining dolphins in captivity, compounded with the very real uncertainty about their value as 'ambassadors' to the species or even to the oceans, ought to be revisited by every prospective patron. While the dolphin entertainment industry may not change overnight, it has progressively been challenged to modify and improve its practices and will surely continue to do so as public awareness about cetaceans increases.

THE DOLPHIN IN LITERATURE

Literature about animals has a tough time competing with film and television, much less live performances, but dolphins have managed to find their way into a number of modern books. While dolphins cannot boast of the kind literary fame achieved by *Bambi, A Life in the Woods, Black Beauty* or *White Fang*, they have had some impact in the literary world. An appropriate place to begin, in the modern era, is Guillaume Apollinaire's quatrain to the dolphin in *Le Bestiaire; ou, Cortège d'Orphée* (1911), which was illustrated by Raoul Dufy. As with many of the poems – each dedicated to a different species – in the collection, the description of the animal reveals more about Apollinaire than the creature itself. The dolphin is described as follows:

> Dolphins, you play in the sea
> But the waves are always bitter.
> Does my joy sometimes burst out?
> Yet life still remains cruel.[7]

To be sure, Apollinaire's work is a bit esoteric, but dolphins had to wait several decades before finding themselves central figures in fiction. The French novelist Robert Merle's *Un animal doué de raison* ('A Sentient Animal', 1967) was translated into English as *The Day of the Dolphin* in 1969 and retained that name for the film of 1973 starring George C. Scott. In *So Long, and Thanks for All the Fish* (1984), the fourth book in Douglas Adams's (1952–2001) remarkably popular 'Hitchhiker's Guide' series of novels, dolphins have abandoned the soon-to-be-destroyed Earth for another dimension, leaving humans behind on a replica of our planet that they have created in a gesture to save humanity. In the novel's reckoning, dolphins are the most intelligent creatures on Earth, just behind mice (who are first) and humans (who are third). Humiliated by years of being treated like circus animals, frustrated by human imbecility in understanding them and

156

aware of the inevitable destruction of Earth, the dolphins leave
the planet for a better world:

> On the planet Earth, man had always assumed that he was
> more intelligent than dolphins because he had achieved
> so much – the wheel, New York, wars and so on . . . But
> conversely, the dolphins had always believed that they
> were far more intelligent than man – for precisely the same
> reasons . . . The last ever dolphin message [warning
> humans of the imminent catastrophe] was misinterpreted
> as a surprisingly sophisticated attempt to do a double-
> backwards somersault through a hoop whilst whistling
> the 'Star Spangled Banner', but in fact the message was
> this: So long and thanks for all the fish.

Having extended his successful series into the 1980s, Adams is
here riffing on the intelligent dolphin paradigm to its fullest,
with a certain degree of wit and irony. These dolphins are so intelligent, Adams suggests, that they are beyond scolding wilfully
stupid humans for poor stewardship of the planet: they simply
pack their bags and go.

While Adams is almost always tongue in check, science fiction
has also given us more earnest novels, such as *The Dolphins of
Pern* (1994), which is the thirteenth book in Anne McCaffrey's
(1926–2011) series *The Dragonriders of Pern*. In this book the world
of Pern has been chosen to relocate humans from Earth, but dolphins are also brought to Pern because of its vast and beautiful
oceans. In this medieval-like world, dolphins (called 'shipfish'
by humans) are meant to work collaboratively with humans,
but ignore them until a chance encounter leads to interspecies
friendship. As a consequence, the humans of Pern recall what
their ancestors knew: dolphins are intelligent and sophisticated

creatures. The dolphins introduce the humans to new technologies (for example, echolocation) and launch the culture in a new and progressive direction.

Despite the almost cartoonish manner in which dolphins are depicted in science fiction, they have not fared very well in the world of comic books. In 1968, however, DC Comics released a comic book called 'Dolphin' (in a *Showcase* issue), in which the main character is a silver-haired woman clad only in a sleeveless shirt and cut-off jeans.[8] Having been abandoned as a child and thrown into the sea, she was rescued by aliens who gave her super-strength and gills (which are never quite visible). She is discovered by Navy divers out on a secret mission, which she ultimately completes on her own. After being nicknamed 'DOLPHIN', she is trained (reflecting contemporary trends with actual dolphins) to speak rudimentary English. The issue concludes in star-crossed love when one of the divers effectively proposes to Dolphin and offers to take her back to 'my land'. But he is rebuffed by his prospective mate who, while certain that land is not for her, is a bit fuzzy about her own identity as an aquatic being: 'Dolphin no go . . . to land . . . must . . . stay here. Chris . . . man. Dolphin . . . only . . . fish.' As a character, Dolphin could apparently not sustain her own title series, although she does make brief appearances in later comics.

Far more successful as a heroic icon was the character Ecco the Dolphin, who was part of a video game developed by SEGA in 1992. One of the mostly widely sold video games of its time, it remains available in a variety of formats. Targeted towards children of about age nine to mid-teens, the game's narrative is very convoluted. Within the game, Ecco must rescue his pod from the evil Vortex aliens who consume the waters of the world every 500 years. As the game progresses, Ecco gains certain powers, including the ability to actually breathe underwater and to use echolocation with laser-like force, thus becoming less like a natural animal than a 'techno-dolphin'. Despite its exaggerated elements (it is a video game after all), Ecco's environmental theme – saving the earth from rapacious forces and restoring natural 'order' – sets it apart from most computer games. Nevertheless, one could hardly call it 'educational', given that players who make it through the game's many layers learn very little about dolphins or the marine environment.

While Ecco is too sophisticated for most children (and, quite frankly, most adults), there are many dolphin toys suited to very young children. The Playmobil company, for example, focuses on dolphins in two of its products, one of which depicts dolphins in an oceanarium and the other (perhaps related) shows two individuals bearing a dolphin in a sling. The idea of dolphins in the wild may not be an idea that sells well with children, and so there is something both domestic and comforting in the Playmobil toy sets, which reinforce containment and control. Still, the toys suggest a narrow model of the human–dolphin relationship that will certainly influence the way children view captivity.

A minor sensation in France was the 2007 song 'Viky le petit dauphin' and the environmentally aware, animated video that accompanied it. In this case Viky is a 'wild' dolphin, although she wears the mask of a superhero and is highly personified. Nevertheless, she encounters all of the perils of the sea, where her mission is to protect the environment, as she explains in the lyrics *'Je viens sauver la planète / Et battre tous les méchants'* ('I come to save the planet / And defeat those who are wicked'). While adults may have found the song and video a little cloying and the character of Viky a little too perky, the masked dolphin found a broad audience among children in France and Belgium. Viky may have had a precursor in the highly stylized representation of a dolphin in *Coucou . . . Les voilà!*, a children's book of

1922 described as 'à la manière de Buffon', in which the illustrator, simply called Marc, provides whimsical but accurate descriptions of animals.[9] 'Of the cetaceans', writes Marc, whose accompanying design illustrates his point, 'the dolphin is the most sympathetic and playful'.

Children's literature, especially non-fiction, has given dolphins their due, but not in any greater number than other charismatic animals. Still, there is a tendency, as one might expect, to cast dolphins in the friendliest and most innocent light possible. The emphasis is typically on dolphin intelligence, and other aspects of their biology and physiology are typically ignored. The dolphin's shape, which even in full-grown adults retains the soft and rounded features that we associate with juveniles, works wonderfully for children.[10]

In 1995 Sergio Bambaren's *The Dolphin: Story of a Dreamer* became enormously popular and sold 1,500,000 copies. Made into an animated film in 2009, the hero of the story, Daniel the Dolphin, leaves his restrictive pod to pursue the purpose of his life. Oddly enough, the 'purpose' is to surf the 'perfect wave', and both readers and viewers are left to wonder whether there might not be bigger issues for Daniel to address than riding a wave for his own pleasure.

A successful series of novels called the *Dolphin Diaries* by the American writer Ben Baglio follows the journeys of thirteen-year-old Jody McGrath (the series is for young adults), the daughter of two cetologists.[11] The family is on a year-long voyage, on the boat 'Dolphin Dreamer', to survey dolphin populations, and while it is never clear what new information is being gathered, Jody finds a dolphin to love in every port of call. The series, to its credit, does attempt to introduce a smattering of dolphin biology and behaviour to the readers, as well as issues such as poaching and the impact of nets. In all, the series touches on

ECCO as depicted in the 2002 instructional manual for the SEGA game.

close to ten species in various works, and while one does not wish to be too hard on Jody or her parents (or the author for that matter), there are very few probing questions about cetology. The bottlenose dolphin, not surprisingly, is at the centre of several novels and appears on almost all of the book covers, including *Beyond the Sunrise* (2004), which focuses exclusively on Irrawaddy dolphins!

Both the Irrawaddy and the Ganges dolphins figure prominently in Amitav Ghosh's novel *The Hungry Tide* (2005), which takes place in the vast mudflats and tidal rivers of the Sunderbans, on the Bay of Bengal. The dolphins are the study subjects of an American-born cetologist named Piyali Roy, who relies on the intuitive knowledge of a guide, Fokir, and the urbane guidance of a professional translator. The beauty of the Sunderbans and its resident dolphins is set against a backdrop of the threatening nature of the forest/swamp itself, which is home to crocodiles, Bengal tigers and huge tidal shifts accompanied by hurricanes. The Sunderbans also bear the scar of the Marichajapi massacre of 1978–9, when Bengali Hindu refugees who had taken up residence in the Sundarbans were forcibly evicted, at the cost of hundreds of lives. In a world riven by natural disasters, predation, political terror, and religious and economic strife, the dolphins are a reminder not necessarily of tranquillity but of the fact that these animals, at least, can outlast the vagaries of catastrophe, whether natural or political.

One of the more striking works to have been written about dolphins is Leó Szilárd's (1898–1964) short story 'The Voice of the Dolphin', published in 1961. Szilárd, a renowned nuclear scientist who played a central role in the Manhattan Project, came to regret (as so many of his colleagues did) his role in advancing nuclear armaments and what later seemed to be an irreconcilable Cold War. In 'The Voice', which projected out into the then-distant

1980s, Szilárd draws on the work of John Lilly to imagine a world where dolphins not only learn the English language but become advanced enough in scientific research to generate ideas – for a group called the Vienna Institute that earned on behalf of the dolphins five Nobel Prizes in Physiology and Medicine. The dolphins invent a new food called Amruss (derived from algae), which in one fell swoop nourishes humans and also controls population growth. They also reach an important international audience through an erudite TV programme, called 'Voice of the Dolphins'. Szilárd depicts tensions in the Middle East that bring the u.s. and ussr to the brink of mutually assured destruction, but the dolphins arrange a conference in Vienna that restores world peace and leads to massive disarmament. At the conclusion of Szilárd's political allegory, the dolphins are killed off by a virus and the Institute itself is destroyed in a fire. In the wake of these events, questions arise about whether the 'voice' of the dolphins was authentically cetacean or merely the initiative of the dedicated scientists at the Institute. Szilárd followed his allegory with the creation of 'The Council for a Livable World' in 1962, which was established to monitor the threat of nuclear war and to warn countries of the escalation in armaments.

The image of the heroic and selfless dolphin gets its comeuppance every now and then. The animated TV programme *The Simpsons* delivers a particularly iconoclastic blow by depicting the revenge of the dolphins on the human race, under the leadership of the dolphin king, Snorky. Lisa Simpson, feeling an irresistible empathy for the captive Snorky, recreates the scene from *Free Willy* as she allows Snorky to escape to freedom. Alas, for Lisa and the other residents of Springfield, the dolphins, now militant and violent, take to the land en masse and banish everyone in Springfield, including Homer, Marge, Bart, Maggie and the well-intentioned Lisa, to a life in the ocean.[12]

Notwithstanding the iconoclasm of *The Simpsons*, the persistent theme in almost all dolphin narratives is their role as golden-age saviours whose intelligence and vision promises a tranquil and peaceful future. In a sense, then, dolphins worldwide have been co-opted by and saddled with the responsibility of recalling an idyllic past and leading the earth to a utopian future. It would be hard to outdo Mette Bryld and Nina Lykke's remarkable analysis of this movement in their book *Cosmodolphins* (1999), which simultaneously skewers New Age thinking about dolphins while offering a rationale for its endurance. 'Playing the part of the noble savage,' Brylde and Lykke observe,

> the dolphin opens the door to a world that promises to redeem our nostalgic longings for a future based in the blissfully innocent lifestyle imagined to have existed prior to techno-civilization. The restored images of the sea as an alluring pastoral source, which in its linkage to womb

and breast also incorporates vivid notions of orality, undoubtedly provide an appropriate setting for symbiotic reconnectedness such as the ones displayed by the noble dolphin.[13]

The 'noble' dolphin, for better or worse, is now a construct that is unshakeable in contemporary Western culture. While it is useful to try to strip away some of the distracting excesses applied to the dolphin in either adulation or ignorance, there is a virtue to holding on to what is – in the big picture of environmentalism – this atypical respect and admiration for a fellow creature.

THE DOLPHIN AS ICON

The image of the dolphin over generations embraces the sublime, sometimes the elegant, and frequently the ridiculous. Seaside towns and port cities often incorporate dolphins into their emblems, and the coat of arms of the city of Brighton and Hove, for example, features dolphins quite prominently. The appeal of dolphins also extends to commercial enterprises, which benefit from the intrinsic appeal of the animal and its graceful shape.

The elegant and lithe form of the dolphin is well suited to ornamental and decorative detail and has served artists well over the centuries. In the seventeenth and eighteenth centuries, designers incorporated the elongated and flexible form of the dolphin into the legs of tables and support armatures of elaborate tableware, from candelabra to epergnes, that distinguished the period. When water was required, as in fountains, pitchers, and vases, dolphin images were sure to be found. Rather than once again employing the conceit of animal paws to accentuate furniture, craftsmen explored the appealingly new form of the dolphin. What is certainly clear is that the form of the dolphin compared

Dolphin handle, from the late 16th century, found on the steam lid of Budapest's Kiraly thermal bath.

to other animals has some distinct design advantages. With other animals, horses for example, designers had to contend with all four legs, which were not only cumbersome in the way that they bent and moved but were also so absurdly thin as to reduce their sturdiness and practicality. Horses, as any amateur artist knows, are difficult to get right; but by contrast, a few short sweeps of line are sufficient to suggest the outline of a dolphin . . . and this has assured the dolphin an ongoing prominence as a design element in the decorative arts.

In early modern Japan, the image of the dolphin added a sense of prestige and strength to objects. The mythical creature, the

Shachihoko, is represented in a number of ways, combining the elements of a tiger and a fish or dolphin. The term *shachi* is used for orcas, and it isn't surprising that Samurai helmets often incorporated the form of a dolphin or killer whale. The image also appears on palace rooftops, for example at Osaka Castle, where it is said to protect the occupants from harm.

One would think the sleek and athletic form of the dolphin would make it a popular mascot in professional sports. But what the dolphin suggests in bodily athleticism is undercut by its mild, indeed happy, facial profile. Without the aggressive and angry facial expressions that make most animal mascots seem threatening, the dolphin may simply be too friendly to be properly fearsome. That said, there are at least two exceptions to this 'rule' worth noting in the world of sports. First are the Miami Dolphins, an American National Football League franchise founded in 1966,

An 18th-century fountain with cover and spigot made of tin-glazed soft-paste porcelain.

Dolphin ceramic tiles, *c.* 1620, made in Holland.

Samurai dolphin helmet, from Japan's Tokugawa shogunate in the 17th century.

A dolphin-like mythical creature, the *Shachihoko*, at Osaka Castle, Japan. The creature was said to offer both prestige and security from fires.

which adopted a bottlenose dolphin – common to the waters surrounding Miami – for the team logo. In the National Hockey League, the Vancouver Canucks employ a logo based on a stylized killer whale, which follows a design from the native Haida peoples. The image appears on both 'home' and 'away' uniforms, which suggests something of its popularity. Their mascot, Fin the Whale, is also a representation of an orca and appears on the team's website and at events as a costumed character. Finally, as a minor exception, it would not do to ignore the Norköpping Dolphins of the Swedish Basketball League, which play in the harbour town of Norköpping to the south of Stockholm.

The logo of the Miami Dolphins football team.

The killer whale emblem of the Vancouver Canucks hockey team.

The endless array of dolphin knick-knacks that crowds the gift shops of virtually every beachfront resort is certainly familiar to most readers. But the popularity of these items, which have no practical function, speaks to the fact that dolphins emblematize a variety of ideas – freedom, spirituality, intelligence, independence, grace and energy – to purchasers, few of whom have actually ever seen a dolphin or know very much about them. Still, with little experience and less knowledge about dolphins, consumers are relentless in their consumption of dolphin images in everything from jewellery to tattoos, where dolphins are among the most requested designs. In contrast to other animals, the distinctive form of the dolphin varies little from species to species, and the absence of facial expressions (beyond the smile) renders the dolphin simpler to interpret as an icon than almost any other beloved creature. The image of the dolphin almost always evokes a sense of *ésprit* and this surely has much to do with its universal popularity.

Where dolphin knick-knacks fit in the contemporary home is another question. Bathroom objects ornamented with leaping dolphins, like children's toothbrushes, bathtub toys and soap caddies, are to be expected, and they can indeed be found in thousands of beachside stores. But the dolphin has also surfaced, as it were, in an unusual personal appliance, intended for adults rather than children: the fact is that one of the most popular 'special' shapes for vibrators is the dolphin. One online site even boasts over 35 different styles of sex toys incorporating images of the dolphin, ranging from the Dolphin Arouser to the Dancin' Dolphin. Sex-toy designers, some of whom may even have an interest in natural history, have obviously found an important muse in the dolphin, which is suggestively phallic in shape and undulating in its movements. But the popularity of the shape may also have something to do with the fact that dolphins – male and female – have been represented as non-threatening and spiritual, and ultimately they have become feminized as both nurturing and sensitive creatures with which it is safe to be intimate.

Where does one go, intellectually, after discussing dolphin-shaped vibrators? Lacking an answer, it may be worth addressing

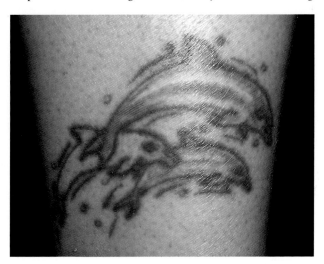

Dolphin leg tattoo.

where animal narratives like this one go in the modern era (to say nothing of the postmodern era). There seems to be an inevitable if not inescapable trajectory for any discussion that involves animals (and the environment) that requires invoking the sublime, the ridiculous and of course, the tragic.

For the sake of this book, one might argue that dolphins are 'truly' sublime, given the widespread adulation they receive, but that sublimity exists in an evolutionary matrix of wonderful complexity in the natural world, where no one species can stand out without at some point foregrounding another. The dolphin is charismatic, but so too is the squid, the mullet, the shark and even the dolphin's wallflower cousin, the porpoise.

The ridiculous is a necessary by-product of our own imaginative capacity in making sense of the animals that surround us. For sheer absurdity, the dolphin vibrator is a good place to start, but so is the ridiculous premise of *Flipper* the television show. No less bizarre are the New Age fantasies that represent dolphins as gifted

Arthur Rackham's illustration of Aesop's 'The Monkey and the Dolphin'.

THE MONKEY AND THE DOLPHIN

172

aliens or re-centred reincarnations of humans. To be sure, such eccentric views are not widely held, but they are prominent enough to inform (and often derail) any conversation about dolphins. In fact, metaphysical narratives about dolphins are inscribed in the cultural zeitgeist at least as frequently as dolphin tattoos are inscribed on physical bodies.

Finally, in a world plagued by over-consumption, environmental neglect and self-interest, tragedy is inevitably linked to almost every creature on the planet. The extinction of the Yangtze river dolphin, one of the largest mammals to disappear in our

David Wynne's sculpture, *Girl with Dolphin*, 1973, near Tower Bridge, London.

lifetimes, should have riveted the world not merely to the plight of dolphins but to the environmental morass in which we are all embedded. By contrast, the impact of the film *The Cove*, at least among Western audiences, was reassuring in that it not only elicited discussion but genuine curiosity, and even action. We

174

are not much closer to solving what Garrett Hardin called 'the tragedy of the commons', but it is hardly necessary to draw sympathetic readers into a familiar lament about the sad realities of environmental degradation.

Instead, I offer a closing reflection about a more intimate tragedy that took place decades ago. As I sat down to write this book, I could not help but recall three dolphins who resided at Montreal's Alcan Aquarium on Île Sainte-Hélène, who were part of a larger group that I studied as an enthusiastic undergraduate. About a year after I moved on to graduate school, a labour strike paralyzed much of the city, including the aquarium, where three of the dolphins, Brigitte, Fanny and Judith, died. After all these years the tragedy of their loss endures. Much of my firsthand knowledge of dolphins was, of course, gleaned from them. I hoped that in the course of writing this book I might be able to come to terms with their captivity, their lives and their unfortunate demise. I do not know that I have, or even that I (or anyone) can make any sense of the fate of these animals, whether wild or captive. What is important, even critical, is that dolphins continue to endure and continue to fascinate us. They are as remarkable, as inspiring and – I hope – as beloved a creature as any other on Earth.

Timeline of the Dolphin

1349

The heir to the French throne is titled 'le Dauphin'

1550s

Konrad Gesner writes his *Historiae animalium*, the first comprehensive zoological texts

1561

Pierre Belon depicts dolphin young and placenta in *The Natural History of Fishes*

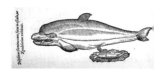

1838

Charles Darwin names the dusky dolphin (*Lagenorhyncus obscures*) after Captain FitzRoy

1881–1914

Tenure of cetologist and classification specialist Fredrick W. True at the Smithsonian Institution

1938

Marine Studios (later Marineland) has first sustained showing of a bottlenose dolphin

1964–1967

Flipper the TV series runs in America

1972

Marine Mammal Protection Act passed by U.S. Congress

1997

International Dolphin Conservation Program Act passed by Congress to eliminate dolphin mortalities in tuna fisheries

. 1585

Amateur Dutch naturalist
Adriaen Coenen compiles
his illustrated manuscript,
'The Whale Book'

1693

English naturalist John Ray
classifies Cetae (i. e. Cetaceans)
as mammals

1804

Bernard Germain de Lacépède
publishes *Histoire des cétacés*

1956

New species identified,
Lagenodelphis hosei, named
Fraser's dolphin after Francis
Fraser, or the Sarawak dolphin

1962

John Cunningham Lilly's
Man and Dolphin argues for
superior dolphin intelligence
and the possibility of language

1963

Flipper the film
is released

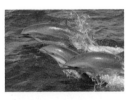

2006

Yangtze river dolphin
declared extinct

2011

New species of dolphin,
the Burrunan dolphin
(*Tursiops australis*),
identified

2012

One of the largest mass strandings
of dolphins (129 common and
Atlantic white-sided dolphins)
in Cape Cod, Massachusetts

References

1 ZOOLOGY AND PHYSIOLOGY

1 George Gordon Byron, 'Childe Harolde's Pilgrimage', *Poetical Works* (Oxford, 1970), Canto IV, verse 29, p. 231.

2 Kristi West, 'Dolphiniaria Dolphin Milk', available at http://nationalzoo.si.edu/SCBI/AquaticEcosystems/Dolphins/Project.

3 The unrelated dugongs and manatees (order Sirenia, family Dugongidae and Trichechidae, respectively), which are often called 'sea cows', also live their entire lives in water. Their evolutionary origins are completely distinctive from that of dolphins and whales.

4 Pliny, *Natural History*, trans. H. Rackham, (London, 1938), book IX, x.33-xii. 36, p. 187.

5 J. G. Thewissen, L. N. Cooper, M. T. Clementz, S. Bajpai and B. N. Tiwari, 'Whales Originated from Aquatic Artiodactyls in the Eocene Epoch of India', *Nature*, CDL (2007), pp. 1190–94.

6 Lara Bejdar and Brian K. Hall, 'Limbs in Whales and Limblessness in other Vertebrates: Mechanisms of Evolutionary Developmental Transformation and Loss', *Evolution and Development*, IV/6 (2002), pp. 445–58.

7 Rudy M. Ortiz, 'Osmoregulation in Marine Mammals', *The Journal of Experimental Biology*, 204 (2001), pp. 1831–44.

8 Alexander J. Werth, 'Odontocete Suction Feeding: Experimental Analysis of Water Flow and Head Shape', *Journal of Morphology*, CCLXVII/12 (2006), pp. 1415–28.

9 Thomas Nagel, 'What is It Like to Be a Bat?', *Philosophical Review*, LXXXIII/4 (1974), pp. 435–50.

10 P. Dejours, 'Water and Air: Physical Characteristics and Their Physiological Consequences', in *Comparative Physiology: Life in Water and on Land*, ed. P. Dejours, L. Bolis, C. R. Taylor and E. R. Weibel (New York, 1987), pp. 3–11.

11 Bejder and Hall, 'Limbs in Whales', p. 451.

12 J. H. Long Jr, D. A. Pabst, W. R. Shepherd and W. A. McLellan, 'Locomotor Design of Dolphin Vertebral Columns: Bending Mechanics and Morphology of *Delphinus delphis*', *The Journal of Experimental Biology*, 200 (1997), pp. 65–81.

13 D. Ann Pabst, 'Morphology of the Subdermal Connective Tissue Sheath of Dolphins: A New Fibre-wound, Thin-walled, Pressurized Cylinder Model for Swimming Vertebrates', *Journal of Zoology*, CCXXXVIII/1 (1996), pp. 35–52.

14 Hiroko Tabuchi, 'Dolphin Reveals an Extra Set of "Legs"', Associated Press (6 November 2011), available at www.msnbc.com.

15 Juliana, Isabella and Craig Hatkoff, *Winter's Tail: How One Little Dolphin Learned to Swim Again* (New York, 2009).

16 Kenneth Stafford Norris, *Whales, Dolphins, and Porpoises*, (Berkeley, CA, 1966), pp. 425–7.

17 William J. L. Felts, 'Some Functional and Structural Characteristics of Cetacean Flippers and Flukes', in *Whales, Dolphins, and Porpoises*, ed. Norris, p. 256; Joy Reidenberg, 'Anatomical Adaptations of Aquatic Mammals', *The Anatomical Record*, 290 (2007), p. 511.

18 See Bejdar and Hall, 'Limbs in Whales', pp. 445–58.

19 Frank Fish, 'Streamlining', in *Encyclopedia of Marine Mammals*, 2nd edn (Amsterdam, 2009), p. 1127.

20 Terrie M. Williams and Graham A. J. Worthy, 'Anatomy and Physiology: The Challenge of Aquatic Living', in *Marine Mammal Biology: An Evolutionary Approach*, ed. Rus Hoelzel (Osney Mead, Oxford, 2002), p. 75.

21 I have termed this behaviour 'surface swim'.

22 Alan Rauch, *The Behaviour of Captive Bottlenose Dolphins (Tursiops truncatus)*, MA thesis, Department of Zoology, Southern Illinois University (Carbondale, IL, 1983), p. 110.

23 Kathleen Maria Dudzinski, Justin David Gregg, Christine Ann Ribic and Stan Abraham Kuczaj, 'A Comparison of Pectoral Fin Contact Between Two Wild Dolphin Populations', *Behavioural Processes*, 80 (2009), pp. 182–90. See also R. Conner et al., 'Coalitions and Alliances in Humans and Other Animals', in *Coalitions and Alliances in Humans and Other Animals*, ed. A. H. Harcourt and F. B. M. Waal (Oxford, 1992), pp. 415–43.

24 Michael Zasloff, 'Observations on the Remarkable (and Mysterious) Wound-Healing Process of the Bottlenose Dolphin', *Journal of Investigative Dermatology*, 131 (2011), pp. 2503–5; published online at www.nature.com/jid/index.html, 21 July 2011.

2 SPECIES OF DOLPHIN

1 K. Charlton-Robb et al., 'A New Dolphin Species, the Burrunan Dolphin *Tursiops australis* sp. nov., Endemic to Southern Australian Coastal Waters', *PLOS ONE*, VI/9 (2011), available at www.plosone.org.

2 Lisa Balance, 'Cetacean Ecology', in *Encyclopedia of Marine Mammals*, 2nd edn (New York, 2009), p. 197.

3 Insa Cassens et al., 'Independent Adaptation to Riverine Habitats Allowed Survival of Ancient Cetacean Lineages', *PNAS*, XCVII/21 (2000), pp. 11343–7.

3 THE DOLPHIN IN HISTORY AND MYTHOLOGY

1 Mark B. Orams, 'Historical Accounts of Human–Dolphin Interaction and Recent Developments in Wild Dolphin Based Tourism in Australasia', *Tourism Management*, XVIII/5 (1997), pp. 317–26, available at www.sciencedirect.com.

2 Louis A. Allen, *Time Before Morning: Art and Myth of the Australian Aborigines* (New York, 1975), pp. 130–33.

3 The website for Pine Mountain Club Real Estate provides brief summaries of Chumash history. At www. pinemountainclubrealestate.com, accessed 23 November 2011.

See also Audrey Wood's retelling of the myth in *The Rainbow Bridge* (San Diego, 2000).

4 Frédéric Laugrand and Jarich Oosten, *The Sea Woman: Sedna in Inuit Shamanism and Art in the Eastern Arctic* (Fairbanks, 2008).

5 'Ganges river dolphin declared national aquatic animal', *Thaindian News* (19 January 2010), available at www.thaindian.com.

6 See R. K. Sinha, S. Behera and B. C. Choudhary's report for the National Ganga River Basin Authority Ministry of Environment and Forests Government of India, 'The Conservation Action Plan for the Ganges River Dolphin 2010–2020. Ministry of Environment and Forests, Government of India' (2010).

7 Samuel Turvey, *Witness to Extinction* (Oxford, 2009); The baiji should not be confused with the Chinese white dolphin, or Indo-Pacific humpback dolphin (*Sousa chinensis chinensis*), which can be found in coastal waters near China, Sumatra and Indonesia.

8 Candace Slater, *Dance of the Dolphin: Transformation and Disenchantment in the Amazonian Imagination* (Chicago, 1994).

9 The film *The Secret of Roan Inish* (1994), directed by John Sayles, depicts a seal who, after transforming herself into a woman, falls in love with a fisherman who has taken her pelt (keeping her in his control). The old ballad 'The Silkie of Sule Skerry' (Child Ballad no. 113) describes a male selkie who has a tryst with a human lover and leaves her to bear his child.

10 Homer, 'Hymn to Apollo', in *The Homeric Hymns: A New Prose Translation*, trans. Andrew Lang (London, 1899), p. 130.

11 J. Z. DeBoer, J. R. Hale and J. Chanton, 'New Evidence for the Geological Origins of the Ancient Delphic Oracle (Greece)', *Geology*, XXIX (2001), pp. 707–10.

12 Aristophanes, *Frogs*, [405 BCE], trans. Paul Roche (New York, 2005), p. 599.

13 Although, as Peggy Noonan has pointed out, the same dolphins that shepherded González's inner tube failed to rescue his mother, who drowned at sea; *Wall Street Journal* (24 April 2000). More recently, the actor Dick Van Dyke has claimed to have been rescued by dolphins: Xan Brooks, 'Porspoises Rescue Dick Van Dyke',

www.guardian.co.uk (11 November 2010).

14 Aesop, *Fables*, trans. George Fyler Townsend [1887] (New York, 1968), p. 35.

15 Cited in L. Harrison Matthews, *The Natural History of the Whale* (New York, 1978), p. 3.

16 Plutarch, *Plutarch's Lives*, vol. v, trans. William Watson Goodwin (Boston, 1874), p. 215.

17 Alan Dugan, *Poems Seven: New and Complete Poetry* (New York, 2001), 'Untitled Poem', p. 300.

18 Lynn Thorndike, *A History of Magic and Experimental Science: During the First Thirteen Centuries of Our Era*, vol. ii (New York, 1923), p. 423.

19 Robert Steele, ed., *Medieval Lore from Bartholomew Anglicus* (London, 1924).

20 T. H. White, trans., *The Book of Beasts: Being a Translation from a Latin Bestiary of the Twelfth Century* (New York, 1984), p. 200.

21 Cited in Thorndike, *A History of Magic and Experimental Science*, vol. ii, p. 505.

22 Mark Twain, *Huckleberry Finn* (New York, 2001), p. 142.

23 Cesare Ripa, *Iconologia; or, Moral Emblems* [1593] (London, 1709).

24 John R. Betts, 'P. T. Barnum and the Popularization of Natural History', *Journal of the History of Ideas*, xx/3 (1959), pp. 353–68.

25 'A Curd from P. T. Barnum: Another Living White Whale at the Museum', *New York Times* (22 November 1861), at www.nytimes.com, accessed 9 March 2012.

26 James E. S. Higham and Michael Lück, *Marine Wildlife and Tourism Management: Insights from the Natural and Social Sciences* (Cambridge, MA, 2008).

27 See Sisco Deen's 'A History of Flagler County', available at www.flaglerlibraryfriend.com/flaglerhistory/flaglerhistory.htm.

4 INTELLIGENCE, SOCIAL BEHAVIOUR AND ECHOLOCATION

1 Donald Griffin, *Listening in the Dark: The Acoustic Orientation of Bats and Men* (New Haven, CT, 1958).

2 Winthrop Kellogg, *Porpoises and Sonar* (Chicago, 1960).

3 Kenneth S. Norris, John H. Prescott, Paul V. Asa-Dorian and Paul Perkins, 'An Experimental Demonstration of Echo-Location Behaviour in the Porpoise, *Tursiops truncatus* (Montagu)', *The Biological Bulletin*, CXX (1961), pp. 163–76; Whitlow W. L. Au and J. A. Simmons, 'Echolocation in Dolphins and Bats', *Physics Today*, LX/9 (2007), pp. 40–45.

4 Kathleen Dudzinski and Toni Frohoff, *Dolphin Mysteries: Unlocking the Secrets of Communication* (New Haven, CT, 2008).

5 J. D. Gregg, K.M. Dudzinski and H. V. Smith, 'Do Dolphins Eavesdrop on the Echolocation Signals of Conspecifics?', *International Journal of Comparative Psychology*, 20 (2007), pp. 65–88.

6 Vincent M. Janik, 'Whistle Matching in Wild Bottlenose Dolphins (*Tursiops truncatus*)', *Science*, CCLXXXIX/5483 (25 August 2000), pp. 1355–7.

7 Lori Marino, 'Cetacean Brains: How Aquatic Are They?', *The Anatomical Record*, 290 (2007), pp. 694–700.

8 Laurie Anderson, *The Ugly One with the Jewels*, sound recording, Warner Bros (Burbank, CA, 1995).

9 Richard Ellis, *Dolphins and Porpoises* (New York, 1989) p. 19.

10 Roger Payne, *Songs of the Humpback Whale* (CRM Records, 1970).

11 Lori Marino et al., 'Cetaceans Have Complex Brains for Complex Cognition', *PLOS Biology* V/5 (2007), p. e139.

12 Ibid.

13 Kevin N. Laland and Bennett G. Galef, eds, *The Question of Animal Culture* (Cambridge, MA, 2009).

14 Luke Rendell and Hal Whitehead, 'Culture in Whales and Dolphins', *Behavioural and Brain Sciences*, XXII/2 (2001), pp. 309–82.

15 C. Guinet and J. Bouvier, 'Development of Intentional Stranding Hunting Techniques in Killer Whale (*Orcinus orca*) Calves at Crozet Archipelago', *Canadian Journal of Zoology*, 73 (1995), pp. 27–33.

16 Diana Reiss and Lori Marino, 'Mirror Self-Recognition in the Bottlenose Dolphin: A Case of Cognitive Convergence', *PNAS*, XCVIII/10 (8 May 2001), pp. 5937–42.

17 Mark Deakos, et al., 'Two Unusual Interactions Between a Bottlenose Dolphin (*Tursiops truncatus*) and a Humpback Whale (*Megaptera novaeangliae*) in Hawaiian Waters', *Aquatic Mammals*, xxxvi/2 (2010) pp. 121–8.

18 Donna Haraway, *When Species Meet* (Minneapolis, 2007); Jacques Derrida, *The Animal That Therefore I Am* [2006], trans. Marie-Louise Mallet (New York, 2008).

19 M. Klinowska, *Dolphins, Porpoises and Whales of the World: The iucn Red Data Book*, World Conservation Monitoring Centre, International Union for Conservation of Nature and Natural Resources, United Nations Environment Programme (Gland, Switzerland, 1991).

20 Tint Tun, 'Sound Signals Used in Castnet Fishing with the Help of Irrawaddy Dolphins', *Bioacoustics*, 17 (2008), pp. 224–6.

21 B. D. Smith et al., 'Catch Composition and Conservation Management of a Human–Dolphin Cooperative Cast-net Fishery in the Ayeyarwady River, Myanmar', *Biological Conservation*, 142 (2009), pp. 1042–9.

22 R. G. Busnel, 'Symbiotic Relationship between Man and Dolphins', *Transactions of the New York Academy of Sciences*, series 2, xxxv/2 (1973), pp. 112–31.

23 Hatteras Jack, a bottlenose dolphin, was said to have piloted ships through the dangerous Hatteras Inlet, North Carolina, in the early nineteenth century. See Jason Cressey, *Deep Voices* (Victoria, BC, 2009), p. 227.

24 Hear Sarah Pirtle's 'Pelorus Jack' on *Two Hands Hold The Earth* (CD, Gentle Wind, 1984); John 'Timberjack' Donoghue, *The Spirit of Pelorus Jack* (CD, Ode, 1973); there is also the early 'Pelorus Jack', words P. Cole, music H. Rivers (1921, http://folksong.org.nz/opo/index.html#Pelorus).

25 The Shark Bay Research Foundation can be found at www.monkeymiadolphins.org.

1 Alexei Barrionuevo, 'Fishermen in Amazon See a Rival in Dolphins', *The New York Times* (16 April 2011), p. A6, available at www.nytimes.com.

2 See the video *Earth Shaker: The Sam LaBudde Story* on Odyseetv.com, at http://vimeo.com/7784773, accessed 8 August 2013.

3 John Kucklick et al., 'Bottlenose Dolphins as Indicators of Persistent Organic Pollutants in the Western North Atlantic Ocean and Northern Gulf of Mexico', *Environmental Science & Technology*, XLV (2011), pp. 4270–77. See also Erin L. Pulster and Keith A. Maruya, 'Geographic Specificity of Aroclor 1268 in Bottlenose Dolphins (*Tursiops truncatus*) Frequenting the Turtle/Brunswick River Estuary, Georgia (USA)', *Science of the Total Environment*, CCCXCIII/2–3 (2008), pp. 367–75.

4 William Gasperini, 'Uncle Sam's Dolphins', *Smithsonian*, XXXIV/6 (2003), pp. 28–30. See also 'Marine Mammal Program' and 'Fleet Systems', available at www.public.navy.mil/spawar/Pacific.

5 Richard C. Paddock, 'Teaching an Old Dolphin New Tricks: Former Members of an Elite Soviet Naval Squad Now Pay Their Way via Circus Shows and Child Therapy', latimes.com (28 September 2000), at http://articles.latimes.com/2000/sep/28/news/mn-28102, accessed 8 August 2013.

6 See 'Iran Buys Kamikaze Dolphins', BBC News (8 March 2000), available at www.bbc.co.uk/news.

6 DOLPHINS AND POPULAR CULTURE

1 See Tors's autobiography, *My Life in the Wild* (Boston, 1979), in which he discusses his change of heart about killer whales (pp. 184–92), leading to the conclusion 'I am against keeping killer whales in captivity' (p. 192).

2 See Civ. No. 14458. Court of Appeals of California, Fourth Appellate District, Division One (19 November 1976), Eckis v. Sea

World Corp. 64 Cal. App. 3d 1, [http://law.justia.com/cases/california/calapp3d/64/1.html, accessed 8 August 2013.

3 See Whale and Dolphin Conservation Society, 'Arguments Against Captivity: Why Keeping Whales and Dolphins in Captivity is Cruel', at www.wdcs.org/submissions_bin/captivityagn.pdf, accessed 8 August 2013.

4 Mike Schneider, 'Killer Whale Kills Trainer at Seaworld as Horrified Spectators Watch', Associated Press (24 February 2010), accessed on www.washingtonpost.com, 8 August 2013. The Occupational Health and Safety Administration (OSHA) imposed a $75,000 fine on SeaWorld. The whale returned to the performance cycle around 2011, until moved to a holding pool for an unspecified illness. Filmmaker Gabriela Cowperthwaite recently released *Blackfish* (2013), a documentary about SeaWorld, Brancheau and Tilikum.

5 Naomi A. Rose, E.C.M Parsons and Richard Farinato, *The Case Against Marine Mammals in Captivity*, 4th edn (Washington, DC, 2009).

6 David Kirby, *Death at SeaWorld: Shamu and the Dark Side of Killer Whales in Captivity* (New York, 2012).

7 Guillaume Apollinaire, *Le Bestiaire, ou, Cortège d'Orphée*, illus. Raoul Dufy (Paris, 1911), translation mine, n. p.

8 J. Scott Pike, 'Dolphin', ed. Dick Giordano, *Showcase*, 1/79 (1968).

9 Marc, *Coucou! . . . Les voilà!* (Paris, 1922), pp. 11–17, translation mine.

10 See Stephen Jay Gould, 'A Biological Homage to Mickey Mouse', in *The Panda's Thumb: More Reflections in Natural History* (New York, 1980), pp. 95–107.

11 Baglio wrote under the pseudonym 'Lucy Daniels'.

12 *The Simpsons*, 'Treehouse of Horror XI', episode 239, aired 1 November 2000.

13 Mette Brylde and Nina Lykke, Cosmodolphins: Feminist Cultural Studies of Technologies, Animals, and the Sacred (New York, 1999), pp. 170–71.

Select Bibliography

Allen, Louis A., *Time Before Morning: Art and Myth of the Australian Aborigines* (New York, 1975)

Au, Whitlow W. L., *The Sonar of Dolphins* (New York, 1993)

—, A. N. Popper and Richard Fay, eds, *Hearing by Whales and Dolphins* (New York, 2000)

Avery, Charles, *A School of Dolphins* (London, 2010)

Baglio, Ben, *Into the Blue* (New York, 2002)

Bates, H. W., *The Naturalist on the River Amazon* (Berkeley, CA, 1962)

Bearzi, Maddalena, *Dolphin Confidential: Confessions of a Field Biologist* (Chicago, 2012)

—, and Craig B. Stanford, *Beautiful Minds: The Parallel Lives of Great Apes and Dolphins* (Cambridge, MA, 2010)

Bekoff, Marc, ed., *The Smile of a Dolphin: Remarkable Accounts of Animal Emotions* (New York, 2000)

Berta, Annalisa, *Return to the Sea: The Life and Evolutionary Times of Marine Mammals* (Berkeley, CA, 2012)

—, and James L. Sumich, *Marine Mammals: Evolutionary Biology* (San Diego, 1999)

Bryld, Mette, and Nina Lykke, *Cosmodolphins: Feminist Cultural Studies of Technology, Animals and the Sacred* (London, 2000)

Caldwell, David K., and C. Melba, *The World of the Bottlenose Dolphin* (New York, 1972)

Connor, Richard C., *The Lives of Whales and Dolphins* (New York, 1994)

Coté, Charlotte, *Spirits of Our Whaling Ancestors: Revitalizing Makah and Nuu-chah-nulth Traditions* (Seattle, 2010)

Cousteau, Jacques, and Philippe Diolé, *Dolphins* (Garden City, NY, 1975)

Cressey, Jason, *Deep Voices: The Wisdom of Whales and Dolphin Tales* (Bloomington, IN, 2010)

Davis, Susan G., *Spectacular Nature: Corporate Culture and the Sea World Experience* (Berkeley, CA, 1997)

Devine, Eleanore, and Martha Clark, *The Dolphin Smile: Twenty-Nine Centuries of Dolphin Lore* (New York, 1967)

Dudzinski, Kathleen, and Toni Frohoff, *Dolphin Mysteries: Unlocking the Secrets of Communication* (New Haven, CT, 2008)

Ellis, Richard, *Aquagenesis: The Origin and Evolution of Life in the Sea* (New York, 2003)

—, *Dolphins and Porpoises* (New York, 1982)

Evans, Peter G. H., *Whales and Dolphins* (New York, 1987)

Folkens, Pieter A. (illustrator), Randall R. Reeves, et al., *National Audubon Society Guide to Marine Mammals of the World* (New York, 2002)

Frohoff, Toni, and Brenda Peterson, eds, *Between Species: Celebrating the Dolphin–Human Bond* (San Francisco, 2003)

Gaskin, D. E., *The Ecology of Whales and Dolphins* (London, 1982)

Gould, Stephen Jay, *The Panda's Thumb* (New York, 1980)

Harrison, R., and M. Bryden, *Whales, Dolphins, and Porpoises* (New York, 1988)

Hatkoff, Juliana, Isabella Hatkoff and Craig Hatkoff, *Winter's Tail: How One Little Dolphin Learned to Swim Again* (New York, 2009)

Herman, Louis, ed., *Cetacean Behavior: Mechanisms and Functions* (New York, 1980)

Herzing, Denise, *Dolphin Diaries: My 25 Years with Spotted Dolphins in the Bahamas* (New York, 2011)

Hoelzel, Rus A., ed., *Marine Mammal Biology: An Evolutionary Approach* (Oxford, 2002)

Hoyt, Erich, *Orca, the Whale Called Killer* (New York, 1984)

Hurley, S., and M. Nudds, eds, *Rational Animals?* (Oxford, 2006)

Kellogg, Winthrop, *Porpoises and Sonar* (Chicago, 1960)

Laugrand, Frédéric, and Jarich Oosten, *The Sea Woman: Sedna in Inuit*

Shamanism and Art in the Eastern Arctic (Fairbanks, 2008)

Leatherwood, Stephen, and Randall R. Reeves, *The Bottlenose Dolphin* (San Diego, 1990)

—, and Randall R. Reeves, *The Sierra Club Handbook of Whales and Dolphins* (San Francisco, 1983)

Lilly, John C., *Communication Between Man and Dolphin: The Possibility of Talking With Other Species* (New York, 1974)

—, *Man and Dolphin* (New York, 1961)

—, *The Mind of the Dolphin: A Nonhuman Intelligence* (New York, 1967)

McIntyre, Joan, *Mind in the Waters: A Book to Celebrate the Consciousness of Whales and Dolphins* (Toronto, 1974)

Mann, Janet, et al., *Cetacean Societies: Field Studies of Whales and Dolphins* (Chicago, 2000)

Meyer, Wilfried, *The Integument of Dolphins* (New York, 2010)

Montgomery, Sy, *Encantado: Pink Dolphin of the Amazon* (Boston, 2002)

—, *Journey of the Pink Dolphins: An Amazon Quest* (New York, 2000)

Norris, Kenneth S., *The Porpoise Watcher: A Naturalist's Experience with Porpoises and Whales* (New York, 1974)

—, et al., *Whales, Dolphins, and Porpoises* (Washington, DC, 1995)

O'Barry, Ric, *Behind the Dolphin Smile* (Chapel Hill, NC, 1988)

Pringle, Laurence, *Dolphin Man: Exploring the World of Dolphins* (New York, 1995)

Pryor, Karen, *Lads Before the Wind: Diary of a Dolphin Trainer* (New York, 1975)

Purves, P. E., and Giorgio Pilleri, *Echolocation in Whales and Dolphins* (New York, 1983)

Rauch, Alan, *The Behavior of Captive Bottlenose Dolphins (Tursiops truncatus)*, MA thesis, Department of Zoology, Southern Illinois University (Carbondale, IL, 1983)

Reiss, Diana, *The Dolphin in the Mirror: Exploring Dolphin Minds and Saving Dolphin Lives* (Boston, 2011)

Reynolds, John E., Randall S. Wells and Samantha Eide, *The Bottlenose Dolphin: Biology and Conservation* (Gainesville, FL, 2000)

Rose, Naomi A., E.C.M. Parsons and Richard Farinato, *The Case Against Marine Mammals in Captivity* (Washington, DC, 2009)

Slater, Candace, *Dance of the Dolphin: Transformation and Disenchantment in the Amazonian Imagination* (Chicago, 1994)

Smolker, Rachel, *To Touch a Wild Dolphin: A Journey of Discovery with the Sea's Most Intelligent Creatures* (New York, 2002)

Thewissen, J.G.M., ed., *The Emergence of Whales: Evolutionary Patterns in the Origin of Cetacea* (New York, 1998)

Turvey, Frank, *Witness to Extinction: How We Failed to Save the Yangtze River Dolphin* (New York, 2009)

Whitehead, Hal, *Sperm Whales: Social Evolution in the Ocean* (Chicago, 2003)

Würtz, Mauritzio, and Nadia Repetto, *Dolphins and Whales: Biological Guide to the Life of the Cetaceans* (Vercelli, 2009)

Associations and Websites

ALLIANCE OF MARINE MAMMAL PARKS AND AQUARIUMS
www.ammpa.org
An international association for marine life parks, aquaria, zoos, research facilities and professional organizations.

AMERICAN CETACEAN SOCIETY
www.acsonline.org
A volunteer organization to protect whales, dolphins, porpoises and their habitats through public education, research grants and conservation actions.

CARDIGAN BAY MARINE WILDLIFE CENTRE
www.cbmwc.org
Dedicated to conserving Cardigan Bay's marine wildlife through education and research.

CASCADIA RESEARCH COLLECTIVE
www.cascadiaresearch.org
Conducts research to aid in management and protection of threatened marine mammals in the Pacific Northwest U.S.

CENTER FOR WHALE RESEARCH
www.whaleresearch.com
Conducts long-term photo-identification study of killer whales in the San Juan Island area of the Pacific Northwest.

CETACEAN ALLIANCE
www.cetaceanalliance.org
Europe-based non-profit network of non-governmental organizations to preserve marine biodiversity and reduce human impact on cetacean populations.

CRRU: CETACEAN RESEARCH AND RESCUE UNIT
www.crru.org.uk
Scottish organization for cetacean welfare, conservation and protection that provides 24-hour veterinary services for sick, injured and stranded individuals.

DOLPHIN CARE UK
www.dolphincareuk.org
Cetacean preservation society primarily for cetaceans in British waters.

THE DOLPHIN COMMUNICATION PROJECT
www.dolphincommunicationproject.org
Conducts research on dolphin communication, social behaviour and cognition, including longitudinal observations of dolphins in Bimini (the Bahamas), Mikura Island (Japan), Roatan (Honduras) and Nassau (the Bahamas).

THE DOLPHIN INSTITUTE
www.dolphin-institute.org
Hawaii-based organization, based at Louis Herman's Kewalo Basin Marine Mammal Laboratory (KBMML), dedicated to the study and preservation of dolphins, whales and other marine mammals.

EUROPEAN CETACEAN SOCIETY
www.europeancetaceansociety.eu
European consortium to gather scientific studies and conservation efforts of marine mammals.

HEBRIDEAN WHALE AND DOLPHIN TRUST
www.whaledolphintrust.co.uk
Dedicated to enhancing knowledge and understanding of
Scotland's cetaceans and the Hebridean marine environment
through education.

IMMRAC: ISRAEL MARINE MAMMAL RESEARCH AND ASSISTANCE CENTRE
http://immrac.org
Dedicated to the study and conservation of cetacean populations that
inhabit the Eastern Mediterranean and the Gulf of Aqaba/Eilat.

INTERNATIONAL MARINE ANIMAL TRAINERS' ASSOCIATION
WWW.IMATA.org
u.s.-based professional association for marine mammal trainers.

IWDG: THE IRISH WHALE AND DOLPHIN GROUP
www.iwdg.ie
Conservation and study of cetaceans in Irish waters.

MARINEBIO.ORG, INC.
www.marinebio.org
Information site about research on cetacean and marine biology in
general.

MARINE CONNECTION
www.marineconnection.org
UK charity to protect cetaceans worldwide, including animals in captivity.

MARINE MAMMAL COMMISSION
www.mmc.gov
The Marine Mammal Commission, an oversight and advisory body,
is an independent agency of the u.s. Government that addresses
domestic and international activities by federal agencies affecting
marine mammals.

MARINEMAMMALRESEARCH.COM
http://marinemammalresearch.com
A collective of researchers and volunteers supporting marine mammal research in Australia.

MOTE MARINE LABORATORY AND AQUARIUM
www.mote.org
An aquarium and research (rescue) centre on Florida's Gulf Coast.

MURDOCH CETACEAN RESEARCH UNIT (MUCRU)
http://mucru.org
Research centre for the study of cetaceans in Western Australia.

NAMIBIAN DOLPHIN PROJECT
www.namibiandolphinproject.com
Conducts research on whales, dolphins and turtles in Namibia and southern Africa.

NATIONAL MARINE MAMMAL FOUNDATION
http://nmmf.org
A non-profit organization based in San Diego and headed by Sam Ridgway that advises and consults on the behavioural, medical and environmental issues related to marine mammals. Works closely with the U.S. Navy.

NOAA FISHERIES OFFICE OF PROTECTED RESOURCES
www.nmfs.noaa.gov/pr/species/mammals/cetaceans
A reliable source for full descriptions of individual species of whales and dolphins.

OCEAN ALLIANCE
www.oceanalliance.org
Founded by Roger Payne, OA focuses on whales and ocean life relating particularly to toxicology, behaviour, bioacoustics and genetics.

OCEAN CONSERVATION SOCIETY
www.oceanconservation.org
Research organization studying dolphin and sea lion foraging.

OCEAN FUTURES SOCIETY
www.oceanfutures.org
Founded by Jean-Michel Cousteau, the OFS is broadly dedicated to ocean awareness.

THE OCEANIC SOCIETY
www.oceanicsociety.org
California-based organization to protect endangered wildlife and preserve threatened marine habitats worldwide.

OPÉRATION CÉTACÉS
www.operationcetaces.nc
Research on whales, dugongs and dolphins in the Coral Sea and South Pacific.

SARASOTA DOLPHIN RESEARCH PROGRAM (SDRP)
www.sarasotadolphin.org
Headed by Randall Wells, the SDRP has conducted long-term studies of dolphin populations and behaviour in Florida.

SARAWAK DOLPHIN PROJECT
www.ibec.unimas.my/SDP2008
Research on coastal dolphins in the South China Sea.

SEA MAMMAL RESEARCH UNIT
www.smru.st-and.ac.uk
Based at the Scottish Oceans Institute at the University of St Andrews.

SEA SHEPHERD CONSERVATION SOCIETY
www.seashepherd.org
A highly visible and proactive organization based in the UK, dedicated
to 'ending the destruction of habitat and slaughter of wildlife in the
world's oceans'.

SHARK BAY DOLPHIN PROJECT
www.monkeymiadolphins.org
Although based in the U.S., the project studies the friendly coastal
dolphins at Shark Bay in Western Australia.

SOCIETY FOR MARINE MAMMALOGY
www.marinemammalscience.org
The dominant professional society in the United States which
publishes the scholarly journal *Marine Mammal Science.*

SOLAMAC: SOCIEDAD LATINOAMERICANA DE ESPECIALISTAS DE
MAMÍFEROS ACUÁTICOS
www.solamac.org
Society of Latin American marine mammal experts, based in Uruguay.

SOMEMMA: SOCIEDAD MEXICANA DE MASTOZOOLOGIA MARINA
Mexican Society for Marine Mastozoology
www.somemma.org
Located at Universidad Veracruzana, which co-sponsors *SOLAMAC,*
the *Latin American Journal of Aquatic Mammals.*

SPANISH CETACEAN SOCIETY
www.cetaceos.com
Conducts conservation efforts in the Atlantic, the Mediterranean and
the Canary Islands.

TARAS OCEANOGRAPHIC FOUNDATION
www.taras.org
Based in Palm Beach, Florida, the foundation sponsors studies
of whales and dolphins.

WHALE AND DOLPHIN CONSERVATION SOCIETY
www.whales.org
An international charitable organization dedicated to the
preservation and welfare of cetaceans.

WILD DOLPHIN PROJECT
www.wilddolphinproject.org
Headed by Denise Herzing, the WDP is a non-profit scientific research
organization that studies and reports on a specific pod of free-ranging
Atlantic spotted dolphins.

Acknowledgements

I am delighted to express my appreciation to Michael Leaman, my editor at Reaktion, and Jonathan Burt, the editor of this series, for their support, their understanding and patience. I am mindful that this book is part of a lifelong interest in dolphins and though much time has passed, it would be ungracious of me not to look back even briefly. In Montreal, the late Gerald Iles, former director of Manchester's Belle Vue Zoo, encouraged my youthful interest in marine mammals and facilitated many Montreal Zoological Society expeditions to the Gulf of St Lawrence. I was also fortunate enough to earn the friendship of two great, critical pioneers of cetology, David and Melba Caldwell, who were very generous to me during my early research visits to Marineland.

While a biology student at McGill University, the professional staff at the 'Alcan Aquarium' were remarkably supportive and engaged, as were faculty staff in the Department of Biology, including – notably – professors Donald Kramer and Peter Grant.

I am indebted to Dr George H. Waring, who not only directed my Master's thesis, but patiently supported me as I worked through the logistics of visiting at least five research sites throughout the state of Florida. George encouraged me with unswerving enthusiasm.

I am always in debt to George Levine, whose love for Darwin and for birds is an inspiration. My appreciation for natural history has benefited from the friendship of Jack Bushnell, a wonderful scholar, writer and naturalist. I was fortunate to find in Richard Grusin another eager naturalist, whose enthusiasm for the outdoors and whose intellect I continue to cherish.

More recently, the animal studies community has been a source of support and encouragement. Nigel Rothfels and Susan McHugh, leaders in the discipline, can never go unacknowledged, nor can Ron Broglio, Erica Fudge, Brent Mizelle, Boria Sax and Cary Wolfe. Members of the MARMAM Listserv have been very helpful as well.

Although the wonderful artist Carl Buell is credited in these pages, his generosity deserves special reference. I have also benefited from correspondence with Jonathan Geisler, Robert Pitman, Hans Thewissen and Randy Wells.

Students in my 'Animals, Culture, and Society' class undertook an early reading of the manuscript of this book and were very helpful, so I thank Samantha Everling, Katherine Hahn, Keisha Hughes, Meagan Inman, Narah Latortue, Daniel Martin, Quinten Ross, Kristen Tranberg and Victoria Welty.

On a more personal and difficult note, the period of writing this book has unfortunately coincided with the cognitive decline of my wife, Amy Dykeman. I have been able to call upon the support of family, friends, and even our ageing terrier, Manny, to help navigate this uncertain path. These include Debbie Childers, Patti Hayes, Diane Leaghty, Nankina McLaurin, Mildred and Davy Nathanson, Riva and Joyce Rauch, and Audrey and Jared Rorrer. Together with Amy herself, who understood my dedication to marine mammals, they played a significant role in the development of this book.

Coren O'Hara, with whom I share a fascination with marine biology, zoology and natural history, has not only been invaluable as a reader but a source of moral and intellectual support throughout this book's lengthy gestation. I can never thank her enough.

Finally, I hope it will not be taken as a cliché to acknowledge the dozens of dolphins with whom I spent many hours. They went by names such as Dal, Mabel, Splash, Suwa and Zippy; and of course, the dolphins whose memory I invoked at the outset: Brigitte, Fanny and Judith. Like every dolphin in the wild or in captivity, these dolphins deserve our deep respect, gratitude and cooperation, as well as our allegiance to them and their habitat.

Photo Acknowledgements

The author and publishers wish to express their thanks to the below sources of illustrative material and/or permission to reproduce it. (Some sources uncredited in the captions for reasons of brevity are also given below.)

Art Resource, N.Y.: pp. 82, 83 bottom (Erich Lessing); Sally J. Bensusan: p.18; DC Comics: p. 145; Professor Wang Ding: p. 68; Adam P. Fagen: p. 99; Juan Carlos Galeano and Jaime Choclote: p. 78; Getty Images: pp. 9 (David C. Tomlinson), 72 top (Marilyn Angel Wynn), 74 (DEA/G.DAGLI ORTI), 80 (Prehistoric), 84 (Roman), 90 (De Agostini), 119 (Dorling Kindersley), 166 centre (Martin Moos); GTA Inuit Marketing: p. 72 bottom; Mark Heine: p. 28; Daniel Kane: p. 52; Koninklijke Bibliotheek, National Library of Denmark: p. 93 top; Kunsthistorisches Museum, Vienna: p. 71; The Metropolitan Museum of Art: p. 167 (Gift of R. Thornton Wilson, in memory of Florence Ellsworth Wilson, 1950 (50.211.125a-c); Money Museum, Zurich: p. 81; Murdoch University Cetacean Research Unit (MUCRU), Murdoch, Western Australia: p. 66; National Football League: p. 170 top left; National Hockey League: p. 170 top right; National Oceanic and Atmospheric Administration: p. 43; Penn State University Library: p. 100; Tomas Petersen, www.sunny-world.org: p. 174; Philadelphia Museum of Art: p. 168 top (Gift of Anthony N. B. Garvan, 1983 (1983-101-169a,b); Bibi Staint-Pol: p. 87; Alan Rauch: pp. 6, 14, 16, 17, 20, 29, 39, 47, 65, 98, 151; Barry Ruderman, www.raremaps.com: p. 86; SeaPics.com: pp. 14 (Masa Ushioda), 53 (Doug Perrine) 54 (Todd Pusser) 55 (Todd Pusser), 57 (Todd Pusser), 58

(Mark Jones), 59 (Doug Perrine), 60 (Thomas A. Jefferson), 61 (Masa Ushioda), 63 (James D. Watt), 67 (Mark Carwardine), 107 (Doug Perrine), 127 (Lori Mazzuca); Southwest Fisheries Science Center, NOAA Fisheries Service, La Jolla: pp. 11 (Robert Pitman), 64 (Cornelia Oedekoven); Hans Thewissen & Carl Buell: p. 25; U.S. Navy: p. 139 (Photographer's Mate 1st Class Brien Aho); Werner Forman Archive: p. 168 bottom (L. J. Anderson Collection); Wildest Animal: p. 106; Zoological Society of London: pp. 10, 50, 94, 102, 114, 128; Shannon Zurell: p. 171.

Index